DWELLINGS

LIVING WITH GREAT STYLE

Stephen Sills and James Huniford
with Michael Boodro

Bulfinch Press
AOL Time Warner Book Group
Boston • New York • London

First Edition

   Library of Congress Cataloging-in-Publication Data

Sills, Stephen (Stephen Maxey).
   Dwellings : living with great style / [by Stephen Sills, James Huniford, and Michael
Boodro]—1st ed.
      p. cm.
Includes index.
ISBN 0-8212-2846-3
   1. Interior decoration—United States—History—20th century. I. Huniford, James
(James Daniel), 1957– II. Boodro, Michael. III. Title.

NK2004.S563 2003
747— dc21

                                                                    2002043909

Bulfinch Press is a division of AOL Time Warner Book Group.
Book design by Hotfoot Studio
Printed in Italy

Dedication

To Kimberly Hull, our treasured colleague and friend,
who for sixteen years has unstintingly bestowed upon us her vision
and unparalleled skills. We could not have done it without her.

ACKNOWLEDGMENTS

Our thanks, first of all, to all our clients, who for twenty years have put their faith in us, and have allowed us to help them create their homes, their most personal spaces. Without their trust and support it would have been impossible for us to develop our talent. We particularly want to acknowledge those who have granted us permission to feature their homes in this book, but it has been a privilege to work with all of them: Suzanne and Stanley Arkin, Eleanor and Andrew Beer, Nicolas Berggruen, Susan and Carl Brazell, Robert Brownlee and William Jordan, Anne Buford, Blake Byrne, Patricia Butler, Marilyn and Myles Cane, Linda Rappaport and Leonard Chazen, Barbara Cirkva and John Schumacher, Mary Beth and Jeffrey Davidson, Brooke and Emilio Ocampo, Susan and Leonard Feinstein, Alberta Ferretti, Bruce Fiedorek, Betsy and James Fifield, Rhonda Graam, Vivian and Timothy Horan, John Howard, Yves Andre Istel, KCD, Betsy and State Lawrence, Debbie Lawrence, James B. Lawrence, Joan and Dr. Paul Marks, Nancy and Peter Meinig, Pamela Moffat, Ellen and Sam Newhouse, Elyse and Michael Newhouse, Priscilla and Gary Page, Jane Pratt, Renee and Mark Rockefeller, Ian Schrager, Keith Scott, Michelle Smith, Clarice and Robert Smith, Michelle Stein, Gary Sumers, Jill Swid, Nan and Stephen Swid, Robin Swid, Seran and Ravi Trehan, Tina Turner and Erwin Bach, Vera Wang and Arthur Becker, Stark and Michael Ward, and Linda Wells and Charlie Thompson.

Our success would not have been possible without the hard work and dedication of our wonderful staff. Many of them have been with us for a long time, many others have moved on, but we appreciate the efforts of all of them, particularly Val Nitkin, Dawn Burcaw, Matilda Abate, and Asler Valero. We have also received help and encouragement of many kinds over the years from countless friends and colleagues. We are grateful for the support and advice of all of them, and owe a large debt of gratitude to Camille Cesare, Tisa Ferguson, John Galliano, Klaus Kertess, Karl Lagerfeld, and Jimmie Lawrence. We especially want to thank Paige Rense for her unequaled recognition and championing of our work. Nan Swid has continuously influenced our creativity with her own. Tina Turner has enriched our lives with her incredible friendship and passion for creating beauty. Anna Wintour was an early and enthusiastic supporter. And we treasure the memory of the wonderful friendship of the late Bill Blass.

Throughout our careers, we have been fortunate in having enormous support from the press. Among those editors and writers who have featured or written about our work, we are indebted to Alexandra D'Arnoux, François Baudot, Hamish Bowles, Dominque Browning, David Colman, Susan Crewe, Karol De Wulf Nickell, Margaret Dunne, Pamela Fiori, Dennis Friedman, Charles Gandee, Wendy Goodman, Lou Gropp, William Hamilton, Minn Hogg, Cathy Horyn, James G. Huntington, Julie Iovine, Françoise Labro, Patrick McCarthy, Marian McEvoy, Sarah Medford, Senga Mortimer, Jeffrey Nemeroff, Nancy Novogrod, James Reginato, Marianne Rohrlich, Mayer Russ, Margaret Russell, Suzanne Slesin, Carolyn Solis, André Leon Talley, Miguel Flores-Vianna, Pilar Viladas, and Donna Warner.

Of course, a project of this nature cannot come to fruition without the support, skills, and knowledge of many people. We want to thank our friend and writer Michael Boodro, and Ellen Newhouse, who introduced us to our publisher, Jill Cohen, whose enthusiasm has transformed the idea for this book into a reality. We thank Kristen Schilo for her deft editing, and Tanya and David Hughes of Hotfoot Studio for their elegant design. Creating this book has been a wonderful collaboration with all of them.

Finally, our deepest appreciation, love, and thanks go to our parents and to our families.

"We shape our dwellings, and afterwards
our dwellings shape us."
— Sir Winston Churchill

CONTENTS

A home that expresses your personal style will reward you with both physical comfort and visual pleasure.

chapter one
Making a Home

Creating a home with great style, one both beautiful and efficient, is no simple task. We expect our homes to work for ourselves and our families yet also function well when we entertain. We want a home to serve as both sanctuary and refuge, but also to respond to all our varied needs: for family rooms, kitchens with the latest appliances, bathrooms with every luxury, home offices full of high-tech equipment. Most of all, we want our homes to express our personal style, rewarding us with both physical comfort and visual pleasure.

Transforming empty rooms into the kind of home that you want is not quick or easy, nor is it without its heartaches and missteps. For most of us, decorating is intimidating. It requires major expenditures and big decisions often made with insufficient information. (How can you predict the impact of twenty yards of a fabric based on only a small swatch? What will a color chosen from a paint chip look like on four large walls? Will that sofa overwhelm the room?) The arcane language used by many design professionals, the proliferation of "to the trade" signs, and the impossibly lush photographs in shelter magazines and books only serve to further mystify the process.

Even for design professionals like us, buying a house and turning it into a home was a long, complex, and difficult process. But after more than twenty years of experience helping others, we have developed a set of principles and guidelines for dealing with what might otherwise seem a huge and daunting task. These same principles can be used by anyone. They apply whether you choose to work with a decorator or not, and whether your home is a small studio apartment or a large house in the country. We know, because we have designed—and lived in—both.

We originally began to think about buying a weekend house outside of New York

The keys to great style are selectivity, judgment, and learning to refine your eye.

The foursquare architecture of the house, opposite and above, is reiterated by the simple rectangle of lawn, with a fountain, which links it to the guest cottage, right.

City about twelve years ago. It was both the fulfillment of a long-standing dream and the start of a complicated and still ongoing process. We looked at more than seventy houses before finding the one we finally chose, and even that was far from perfect. It was not the stone house we had been searching for, but clapboard. It cost a lot more money than we had been planning to spend, it was in bad condition, and it came with a lot more land, thirteen acres, than we wanted, which would mean a lot more maintenance, as well. But it was also very private and had great bones and nice big boxy rooms. It had the potential to become someplace special.

Great style has nothing to do with your income level. The keys are selectivity, judgment, and refining your eye. All of this comes with experience. Style is important no matter how much money you have—or don't have—to spend.

In the beginning our style was considered fresh, with lots of light and monochromatic color schemes. We were noted for our honey-gold colors, spareness, and lots of breathing room. That was by choice, but in reality, it was also a matter of economics. In truth, we didn't have a lot of money for antiques, expensive fabrics, rugs, and heavy draperies. For our own apartment, we literally found chairs on the street. But then we covered them in a beautiful mohair fabric. Our look was definitely a matter of choice, but the style evolved under certain economic conditions.

From living in small spaces we learned about scale and the importance of bringing light into rooms to enhance and enlarge them. We stress the importance of editing, function, and order. No extra tables or chairs. Even the closets need to be edited and organized.

The renovation of our country house occurred in three stages. The first involved painting the house all white, inside and out, and staining the floors the color of gray driftwood. We made the outside monochromatic by painting all the shutters and trim the same pale gray, which gave the house a more sculptural presence on the land. On the first floor, we replaced many of the windows with French doors to bring in more light and to make the ceilings appear higher. After creating this neutral background, we were able to move in.

During the second stage, while living in the house and really learning how we used the space, we focused on the guesthouse. This involved major structural repairs, such as putting in new insulation and electrical work and redoing the roof. We transformed its ground-floor space into one large room to give immediate access to the outdoors, installed a cobblestone floor to further the feeling of being outside, and put in a kitchenette for outdoor entertaining.

For the third and final stage, we returned our focus to the main house. We laid stone floors throughout the ground floor. We had wanted a stone house for its charm and patina. Now, with stone floors, we got the same feeling. Terraces were built off several rooms, which not only made the rooms appear more spacious, but provided another tactile surface and connected the house more directly to the outdoors.

The original kitchen was huge, designed to be used by servants. Since we didn't need a large formal dining room and a porch, we converted those spaces into one big central library: a space to read, watch TV, or serve an informal dinner. By breaking up the kitchen, we were also able to create a small dining room for intimate weekend dinners. A prime concern was creating a larger and more dramatic entry hall. We took out the elevator and coat closet to enlarge the space and expanded the opening into the living room.

To make a house fit your needs, you first have to know what your needs are. To create a home that reflects your taste, you have to analyze your style and determine what you love.

This book is designed to help you understand those needs and to give you the information and inspiration necessary to create a home that will bring you pleasure for years to come.

Editing, function, and order are important

In the guest cottage, rough meets refined in the mix of cobblestone floors, a Louis XVI gilt tester bed, and a Regency traveling money-changing cabinet.

for any room.

A prime concern was creating a larger and more dramatic entry hall.

The entry contains a painting by Agnes Martin whose shape is echoed by a seventeenth-century Italian marble bowl holding an eagle's nest of barbed wire. Seventeenth-century marble columns from Cairo frame an English candle stand from Kew Gardens. Inset: On the opposite side of the entry stands a Louis XVI neoclassical oak cabinet.

We converted a formal dining room and porch into a central library for reading, watching TV, and informal dinners.

The view from the library into the living room, above. The étagères are Directoire and hold Giacometti lamps. The sphinx table beyond is an eighteenth-century copy of a Roman marble in the British Museum. A small dining room, opposite, is used for intimate weekend dinners. The table and chairs are Louis XVI; the chandelier is by Giacometti.

Discovering your personal style is the crucial first step in creating a beautiful home.

chapter two
Finding Your
Personal Style

Discovering your personal style and devising the possible expression of the way you want to live are both daunting challenges and exhilarating adventures. They require rigorous self-examination, an array of decisions both major and minor, a willingness to edit, and far more choices and possibilities than you could ever imagine. The process can be as exhausting as it is exciting, but it is the crucial first step in creating a beautiful home.

Perhaps no other endeavor will expose you to so many options, materials, and choices. The sheer array of products—from doorknobs to dressers, finials to fine art—in the marketplace today can overwhelm even the most seasoned design professionals. Before proceeding, you need to put your taste to the test. The answers you discover will not only make the process easier, they will enrich your life as a whole. And whether you hire a decorator or decide to design your living space yourself, you will not make the same mistakes so many people do and end up with a home that looks like those of their friends, but that in no way satisfies their real needs and desires.

Determining what you love and need is a three-step process. The first step is to analyze your needs, the second is to determine your budget, and the third is to scrutinize your desires. Surprisingly, the first two are much easier than the last.

To determine what you need from your home, think about how you really live each day, and not necessarily how you want to live. Do you have a big family? Young children? Do you live alone? Do you entertain often? Do you usually do so with large cocktail parties, or small dinners? Are the dinners formal or casual? All of these factors determine how your house should function. Your home also needs to reflect the various stages in your life. A house with young children has to answer very different needs from one with teenagers. No single solution

It is your

personality that

brings a room

alive.

Refined and rustic meet in a house in the South of France. Roman Attic vases line the living room mantel, opposite. An Indian traveling trunk holds an Etruscan Attic vase and an Art Nouveau sculpture, right.

In our office, a wall is filled with a changing array of favorite photographs, postcards, and pages torn from magazines.

will be appropriate for all stages of your life. Change is the essence of life, and it should be reflected in your home.

Understanding your needs also requires you to analyze how you use each room. Do you live in a small apartment where one room must answer all your needs? Do you have a large house with a formal living room? Or is your living room multifunctional, the place where you also watch television and spend time with your family? Do you have a separate dining room, or does dining take place in a room with another function, such as a library or den? Does your kitchen serve as a family gathering spot as well as a place for cooking and eating? Is your library used as a home office, or even a guest room on occasion? Are the bathrooms shared or are they private refuges? The answers will determine how you approach the decor of each room.

Once you understand your needs, you can devise a budget you feel comfortable with. You have to truly understand the costs involved. If your budget is not large, it may be necessary to decorate in stages. It is always better to do well what you can afford, and to do it in steps, than attempt to do a whole project on an inadequate budget and cut corners. You will never be happy with the results.

After determining your needs and budget comes the most difficult part—deciding what you really love and what you

want your home to be. We all have a broad array of objects, periods, styles, and colors that we like and respond to, but selecting those we really want to live with on a daily basis, and to spend time and money on, is a difficult process. When it comes time to put your money down and make a choice, how modern are you at heart, or how traditional? Many people have made expensive mistakes, giving in to whims or fashion, being persuaded by friends or salesmen or decorators to indulge in objects or colors or shapes that do not truly reflect their tastes. How do you prevent this?

First, develop a tool that virtually every professional designer uses, and create a file or, better yet, a bulletin board of "inspirations." Clip photographs from magazines or newspapers of things you really love. And don't confine yourself only to photographs of rooms. Use pictures of paintings, scraps of fabrics, postcards of works of art. Accumulating these images and looking at them carefully, deciding which details you really like and which elements you don't, can be inspiring as well as instructive. Don't be afraid to look carefully and really be honest about your responses. Do the same with the homes of your friends, public spaces, or even restaurants. Which elements do you respond to or even covet? What do you think are mistakes?

Go to museums and look at paintings. The colors and shapes in works of art that

In a Fifth Avenue apartment, we needed to accommodate both family life and a museum-worthy collection of modern art. In the entry, left, optical-illusion marble flooring is centered by a Jean-Charles Moreau table and a neoclassical German chandelier. In the living room, below, a custom sofa, an Empire center table, and Russian neoclassical chairs create a rhythm of curves throughout the room.

Each client is unique, and fortunately, most do not want a "signature" style imposed on them.

The library, left, features custom bookshelves flanking an English mantel. The lattice-back chair is Austrian. A view from the entry to the living room, opposite, illustrates how the colors and curves of the furniture were inspired by the Lichtenstein painting.

you love can be a telltale sign of the direction your decorating should go in. Do you prefer Roy Lichtenstein or Brice Marden? Force yourself to choose only one section to visit. Would it be the Greek and Roman wings, the Impressionists, or the contemporary galleries? If you could bring home

and its placement within the room. Would you choose English Chippendale furniture or modern French pieces? American country or Gustavian Swedish? Are there any styles that make you feel either uncomfortable or particularly at home? What is it specifically that you respond to?

only one painting, would it be a Renoir, a Cézanne, or an Ellsworth Kelly? Look at the period rooms. Which do you find most attractive? Which could you perhaps see yourself sitting in and having a cup of tea? Look at the forms and scale of the furniture

Another trick is to look in your own closets for clues. Do they hold more dressy items than casual ones? Are there more jeans than suits? What are the colors? Are there more browns and dark colors than pastels? Are there more tweeds than florals,

Personal quirks

give a room its

In a Manhattan apartment, chairs by Ruhlmann and a 1940s Swedish table with a sculpture by Botero. Opposite: A Calder wall sculpture and a screen by Eileen Gray. The sofa is from our furniture line, Dwellings.

No other creative endeavor will expose you to so many options, materials, and choices.

human qualities.

Two very distinct dining rooms. In a downtown Manhattan apartment, opposite, American ladderback chairs and a collection of photographs are offset by a whimsical American iron chandelier and sheer cotton damask shades. In an uptown apartment, right, English chairs surround a French nineteenth-century table. Striped walls give the illusion of height.

solids than patterns? What are the fashion mistakes you've made over the years, the pieces you rarely wear, and which are the items you reach for repeatedly? All of this information can help you decide what colors to use in your home. Do you prefer sun colors or ice blues, earth tones or bright primaries? Do you like vivid contrasts or a subtle range of shades and textures?

If your wardrobe consists largely of jeans and T-shirts, for example, you will probably feel most comfortable with casual cotton upholstery and fabrics that are breezy and fresh, not formal silks and velvets. If your closet is full of tailored suits, you would probably opt for tailored and streamlined furniture covered in more luxe materials.

Also, where you travel and the kinds of objects you bring home from your travels can be quite revealing about what you truly love. Do you prefer Scandinavia or Italy? Would you choose England or Russia? Would you be happier in southern Florida or northern Maine? Do you collect Provençal pottery or New England folk art? Do you collect mirrors or miniatures, Chinese porcelains or majolica? Vintage linens or antique watering cans? Candlesticks, boxes, rocks and crystals, or movie posters? The items you love not only should be incorporated into the design of your home, they can be a very good indication of the kind of decoration that is ideal for you.

Don't be afraid to take a hard look at the way you live now. We always try to see a client's current living space before we start a project. Each client is unique, and fortunately, most do not want a "signature" style imposed on them. Our job is to create a home that reflects their tastes and dreams. Seeing their present homes, and the successes and failures therein, can be crucial to understanding what we and the client are attempting to achieve together.

Even if you are not happy with your current space, it can be revealing. Do you live with simple, clean lines, or do you prefer more traditional furniture? Do you gravitate toward tailored and meticulous upholstery, or do you prefer loose-fitting slipcovers and overstuffed, unconstructed pieces? Do you like matched and coordinated accessories, or a cluttered, eclectic mix? Are you the kind of person who can't stand it if a picture frame is crooked on the wall? What annoys you can be as telling as what you love. If you are neat and precise, you will want to ensure that you have lots of storage. If you love to lounge, you will want to be surrounded by soft, richly textured fabrics.

Give yourself a quiz. Do you prefer high heels or flat shoes? Do you prefer a formal French garden or an English cottage garden? While no one should be boringly consistent, and none of us feels the same way all the time, the answers can be informative and helpful.

A still life in a Manhattan apartment contrasts the gleam of wood and glass.

An upstate New York country house
with its original oak plank flooring is
updated with dyed plaster walls, a
French iron chandelier, and a sofa and
coffee table by Dwellings.

*The more you understand and accept your own
personality and tastes, the more
successful your rooms will be.*

QUIZ

Here is a simple quiz that might help you begin to understand your personal style. Try to answer the questions honestly but also impulsively. Trust your instincts, a process that will become more important as you refine your understanding of your tastes. Be sure to answer all questions, even those that you think don't immediately apply.

If hosting a dinner party, you would serve:
  a. beef Wellington
  b. tandoori chicken
  c. sushi

If you could take a free trip anywhere in the world for a week, you would choose:
  a. Paris
  b. Marrakesh
  c. Montana

To fill a vase, you would choose a bouquet of:
  a. peonies
  b. daisies
  c. tulips

For a special evening out, you would select:
  a. the opera
  b. a Broadway play
  c. a rock concert

Your preferred postwar artist is:
  a. Francis Bacon
  b. Roy Lichtenstein
  c. Brice Marden

When choosing a new suit or dress you would look first at:
  a. Ralph Lauren
  b. Christian Dior
  c. Marc Jacobs

If given $2,000 in mad money, you would purchase:
  a. a Chinese porcelain bowl
  b. a pre-Columbian artifact
  c. a print or drawing by a young artist

When renting a classic movie, you would be most likely to choose:
  a. *Gone With the Wind*
  b. *Some Like It Hot*
  c. *2001: A Space Odyssey*

Your dream dog (one you'd never have to care for) would be:
  a. a beagle
  b. a Dalmatian
  c. a greyhound

Your favorite sport to watch is:
  a. tennis
  b. basketball
  c. skiing

ANSWERS

If the majority of your answers were:

a. You are a traditionalist. This does not necessarily mean that you prefer only Queen Anne furniture or Chinese porcelains, but that for you, the classic and elegant take precedence. Whether you like Chippendale or Jean-Michel Frank, you want to be surrounded by the best, and lots of it. You are seeking a sense of permanence in your home and don't worry about showing off or impressing others. Any object that you love takes on value for you, and nothing shouts for attention. You are at ease with yourself and your home but need to be careful not to shut yourself off from new ideas and influences.

A corner of a New York living room is proof that it is possible to create harmony with colors and patterns that don't necessarily match.

b. You are eclectic in your tastes and are open to new influences. You value comfort in your home and like to entertain casually but don't want to become predictable. You might enliven a basic white room with vivid shots of color, or mix neo-Gothic chairs with over-stuffed upholstery. For you, surprise is important, and you like to keep people guessing. But because your tastes are so wide and encompassing, it will be hardest for you to edit them to create the sense of a cohesive whole in your home. You have to realize that you can't express all your tastes in one room.

c. You are a purist. For you, only the newest, most pared-down, and even futuristic style will do. You prefer monochromatic and subtle color schemes and clean lines, whether in ancient Chinese furniture or Philippe Starck plastic. Roman antiquities and high-tech minimalism are both pleasing to your eye. You have a passion for what is new and for what comes next. But you shouldn't let this dominate your design process. Remember, a home is more than a showcase for what is new or unusual; it is also important that it be functional and comfortable for you, your family, and your friends.

Of course, this quiz is simply an exercise and should be taken in a spirit of fun. Hopefully, it will get you thinking about what you truly admire and respond to, and that is the most important first step in creating a home.

Above all, be honest with yourself. What you like in the abstract (or in small doses) can be quite contrary to your true inner personality, and it can be a disappointing, time-consuming, and expensive mistake to try to fool yourself into believing, for example, that you're more avant-garde than you really are, or more adventurous. Even what you think of as your weaknesses can be made into strengths, but only if you acknowledge them and work with them. Even if you have been brought up on modernism, you may be more traditional than you want to admit—or vice versa.

And don't be afraid to accept, even embrace, the complexities and contradictions of your personality, for it is these that will give a room true depth and character. Just because you wear custom-made suits doesn't mean you can't dance to Bruce Springsteen. A room that is in perfect balance, with proper proportions, harmonious colors, and exquisitely tasteful style can be the most sterile and staid room you have ever seen. It is the personal quirks and touches that give a room its human qualities. A room needs to be a little off, and a little surprising, to give it life, to keep it from becoming cold and corporate. So indulge in your quirks, even accentuate them. If you collect antique toys, put them out for the world to see. It is your personality that brings a room alive. The more you understand and accept your own personality, your own tastes, and your own style, the more successful your rooms will be.

In a country house, a Victorian tufted chair upholstered in nubby white linen is contrasted with colorful American rag rugs.

Only after you understand how you will use a room are you ready to devise a floor plan.

chapter three
Planning a
Room

Great rooms are created from the ground up—literally. Devising a floor plan is the essential first step in creating rooms that are comfortable, functional, and beautiful. It is impossible to overemphasize its importance. With space at a premium, and rooms increasingly taking on more than one function, a flexible, practical floor plan is even more critical.

The way we use rooms has changed greatly in the past two decades. Partly this is a result of technology, ranging from fax machines to the Internet, from wide-screen televisions to cellular phones. But it is also a function of the changes that have affected couples and families. More people are living on their own than ever before, but there are also greater numbers of extended families that live together at least for part of the year. People increasingly are working at home and most need an adjunct home office. People tend to entertain less frequently and do so more casually than twenty or even ten years ago. All these factors should be taken into consideration when rethinking exactly how you will use your rooms.

People have been moving away from formal living rooms that are used more for display than living, adopting the European method of actually using the living room. This means a shift away from decorating with silks and brocades that are too precious for everyday living to using fabrics that grow more beautiful with age, such as leathers and velvets. In smaller apartments and houses, the formal dining room has given way to a combined library/dining room. Often a guest bedroom also has to function as an office or a den. The plan must accommodate these dual functions.

Today, the rooms we use most tend to be the kitchen, the bath, and the bedroom. The latter two are private refuges, the former the place where we not only cook but also increasingly commune with family

members and guests. Baths become spas, with elaborate Jacuzzis and multihead showers, dual sinks, steam rooms and saunas, vanity tables, and even exercise equipment. Bedrooms and baths are now being stocked with such luxuries as small refrigerators, coffee machines, and elaborate entertainment systems.

And with the popularity of video games and the rise of the Internet, the television is becoming ever more ubiquitous. In the future, the centrality of the TV and/or computer screen is likely only to continue. In fact, a media room, often serving as a transitional space between the kitchen and living room, stocked with computer, stereo, DVD, and fax machine as well as television, is the new "rec room."

Once you understand how you will use a particular room, you are ready to work out a plan. Make a written list of all the activities the space must accommodate so that all factors are considered. Next, look at the room itself. What is its position within the larger space? Does it serve as a primary

Working out a floor plan at the beginning not only helps prevent expensive mistakes, it can also unleash your creativity.

In the large room are two distinct seating areas bridged by an Empire center table.

In a Manhattan apartment, a library/media room that is used every day had to be both practical and elegant. The chairs are by Hoffmann, the table by Dunand. The sofa is by Dwellings. The bookcases, opposite, were inspired by Mondrian. The harlequin carpeting is a custom design.

Make a written list of all the activities a room must accommodate so that all factors will be considered.

destination and resting spot, or is it a transitional space, more path than place? Where are the doors and windows? What are the traffic patterns? Is there an adequate flow through the rooms, or are there physical and visual dead-ends, where people

tinguished, you may want to create a room that looks inward, or toward another focal point, such as a fireplace or an alcove. What are the room's proportions and ceiling height? These will dictate not only the scale of furniture but even the mood of the room.

will get stuck, where the eye comes to an abrupt halt? What kind of light does the space get during the day? What are its exposures or views? If the views are wonderful you will probably want to keep the windows clear of furniture, so that you can walk up to them. If the views are undis-

Space is the ultimate luxury, so be certain to use what you have carefully and well. Your plan should take into consideration a room's weaknesses as well as its strengths. In the United States, there are very few perfectly proportioned rooms, whereas in France it is difficult to find a badly proportioned one.

Always keep in mind the traffic pattern, the flow of people into and out of a room.

Sightlines should be open and engaging.

The main room of our guest cottage, right and previous pages, is designed for maximum flexibility and can also be used for large luncheons or dinner parties. Regency sofas are lined up against the wall, the ottoman can be used as seating or as a low table, and the sixteenth-century Italian table can also function as a buffet. Pre-Columbian ax handles in an Italian tazza create a still life on the floor.

But by taking problems into consideration at the beginning, it is much easier to disguise them or even transform them into strengths. We often have to work with rooms that have unusual proportions, such as an off-center fireplace or low ceiling, windows that are not symmetrically placed, or rooms that are misshapen.

Even these drawbacks can be used to advantage. A flaw can become a focal point. If a room is misshapen, with a cut-off corner, for example, you may decide to set the whole arrangement of furniture at a diagonal, to emphasize the corner. If ceilings are low, keep window treatments to a minimum. Elaborate curtains require soaring heights and look ridiculous and overbearing in a low space. But tailored, trimmed-down curtains or simple blinds or shades can be mounted right at ceiling level to give the illusion of height. If your space is small, don't make the mistake that so many people do and fill it with oversized furniture. We have never gone along with the popularity of overstuffed sofas and chairs. As far as we are concerned, there is nothing more beautiful than small-scale furniture. But always remember that you will need at least one large, comfortable chair to sit in. That doesn't mean you need a huge chair-and-a-half, however.

Always keep in mind the traffic pattern, the flow of people into and out of a room. People should not walk into a room and be stopped by the back of a sofa or a table, for instance. Sightlines should be open and engaging. The visual field should be clear—another reason to minimize the amount of large, heavy upholstered pieces. Small, low, and movable furniture pieces are often preferable—benches and ottomans and petite slipper chairs, for example. Not only do such lightweight pieces increase the flexibility of a room and make it easy to create different configurations depending upon need, they are also less visually heavy and allow the eye to move freely around the space. Generally, windows should be accessible and entry and exit points should be clear, to prevent any sense of claustrophobia. If you do a lot of entertaining, it is usually wiser to break up a large space with multiple seating areas. This will bring scale to a large space, and provide opportunities for intimacy.

Planning is equally important in other rooms. For obvious reasons, it is important to minimize the walking distance between appliances in kitchens. The kitchen should be laid out so that cooking is a pleasure, both storage and counter space is maximized, and doors of cabinets, refrigerator, oven, and dishwasher don't interfere with each other when open.

For a showhouse room inspired by the singer Tina Turner, we created a glamorous but modern setting that would play off the room's elegant paneling. The sconces are by Andre Arbus.

Unusual proportions, an off—center fireplace,
low ceilings, asymmetrical windows — even these drawbacks
can be used to advantage.

In the bedroom of a country house, a vibrantly striped French carpet adds a sense of expansiveness and shifts the eye away from the low ceiling. The cabinets flanking the fireplace are American and originally held type in a printing shop. The zebra-wood desk and the ratchet chair are both French, from the 1940s. The bed is nineteenth-century American.

In bedrooms, you should not walk in and be immediately confronted by the bed. In small bedrooms it can be difficult to keep the bed from being the focal point, but bedrooms are much lovelier when a beautiful chest of drawers or a seating area is the initial focus. In small rooms, you may want to put the bed against the same wall as the door, in order to keep from walking into it, or set it at an angle in a corner.

Many people feel that creating and manipulating a to-scale floor plan is a difficult and abstract task, but it is actually quite simple. Not only will your floor plan help prevent expensive mistakes—furniture that turns out to be too big for the room, pathways that are too narrow, seating arrangements that are confining and claustrophobic, for example—but it encourages experimentation and will often inspire you to come to a solution you might never have thought of otherwise. Even a simple plan, drawn on tracing paper to a scale of one inch to a foot, with windows and doorways clearly marked, can be an invaluable tool. Small pieces of paper cut out to the same scale can serve to represent your major items of furniture, and you can move them around to create various layouts. (This is certainly easier than moving the pieces of furniture themselves.) Or if you prefer, place tracing paper over the room template and sketch possible arrangements. If you are able to work directly in the empty room, one trick is to cut pieces of newspaper to the actual dimensions of your furniture and move them around on the floor.

Of course, floor plans cannot re-create the scale and volume of furniture. Sometimes you can simulate scale by using several dining chairs lined up and covered with a sheet to indicate a sofa. It can also be difficult to show changes in level on a floor plan, such as a sunken living room or platforms. And floor plans cannot indicate the effects of lighting, although when drawing up your plan, make certain that there are adequate electrical outlets on every wall so that you will have maximum flexibility later. Before decorating begins is the time to call in an electrician if necessary.

Because drawing up a floor plan makes you focus on a room's room's strengths and weaknesses, it may inspire you to implement a few structural changes as well. You may decide to widen an entryway, for example, or raise the height of a doorway. Though this can be frustrating and expensive, it is far better to make these changes early on, rather than continue working on a room you will never be happy with.

Obviously, there can still be surprises when a floor plan is converted into three dimensions. But despite their fallibility, plans are still valuable. Working one out at the very beginning not only helps prevent expensive mistakes, it can also help unleash your creativity.

Space is the ultimate luxury, so be certain to use what you have carefully and well.

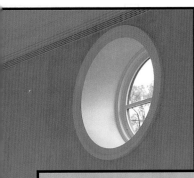

Multiple seating areas bring scale to a large space and provide opportunities for intimacy.

The main room of a midwestern home has multiple seating areas with movable chairs and a parchment center table. A pair of English George I gilt tables are used rather than a coffee table. The sofa is a custom design.

Small, low, and movable furniture increases the flexibility of a room and allows the eye to roam freely around the space.

The dining room, opposite, contains two square dining tables that can
be pulled together. For very large parties, a third can be brought in to seat
as many as twenty-four. The French dining chairs are by Sue et Mare, from
the 1930s. In the library, above, are multiple seating options. The chandelier
is French-Moroccan, the mirror is Italian Baroque. The windows are left
accessible to promote the views.

In the beautifully proportioned living room of a Manhattan apartment, symmetry is emphasized by a pair of English Regency mirrors and the matching urns on the mantel. But the sofa and upholstered chairs are placed off-center.

The walls of our Manhattan apartment are
stenciled and a plaster cornice was installed.
The sofa and chair are Dwellings, the stool is
by Jean-Michel Frank. The bed, opposite, is
placed at an angle to make it more accessible.
It is surrounded by favorite drawings and a
painted French Empire chair.

A room's function should be paramount in determining the way it looks.

chapter four
Living in a Room

Creating a floor plan is only the first step. Numerous other elements—from lighting to furniture selection to the choice of colors—will affect how well a room functions. All these decisions together will determine whether or not a room is visually appealing and welcoming.

If you consider all of these elements at once, it is easy to become overwhelmed. But if you think in terms of specifics—What are the strengths and weaknesses of this particular room? What do I need it to accomplish? What is the mood I want to evoke?—it becomes much easier to face the many aesthetic and functional questions that inevitably arise.

As examples, we want to discuss three very different rooms we have created. The principles behind the design of each remain the same, and the questions we asked while undertaking their creation were identical, but the answers, and the solutions they suggested, could not have been more varied.

A ONE-ROOM APARTMENT

The first is the studio apartment, nicely proportioned but small, where we started our business in Manhattan. The room had only two windows, but there was abundant light and plenty of lovely details, including a fireplace with a beautifully carved mantelpiece. The space had to serve as both our home and office.

We had to make the space as flexible as possible, maximize storage, and create a functional plan with movable pieces that could perform multiple functions. We also did not want to have to resort to the dreaded pull-out sofa bed. We needed to devise something that could serve as a sofa during the day and a comfortable bed at night, without any arduous transformations. We wanted a functional space but also one that was elegant, comfortable, and relaxing.

To make the space seem larger, we chose a monochromatic palette of rich golden creams and pale beiges, used on

visual cornice, which lifted the eye and made the ceilings seem higher.

To maximize storage we placed two fabric-draped tables on each side of the bed, both of which hid storage (a chest of drawers and shelving) underneath. All the other furniture was movable and small in scale and served several functions. A drum table, for example, contained shelves, so that it could hold books within as well as drinks or a lamp on top. And all the furniture, with the exception of a few small dark wood pieces to provide contrast, was kept within the same restrained color scheme.

A monochromatic palette of rich golden creams and beiges makes the space seem larger.

the walls, in the upholstery, and even on the windows. We hung several mirrors to visually enlarge the space and to spread the golden light throughout the room. To make the ceilings seem higher, we hung the curtains at ceiling height, above the windows, and used striped shade fabric to emphasize the vertical. We also hung the pictures at a higher than normal level, to lift the eye.

We were fortunate that the room already had a focus in its centered fireplace. The mantel became a landscape of similarly colored objects, and we took a decorative motif from the carvings on the mantel and stenciled it high on the walls as a kind of

None of the items in the room was grand or expensive. We owned no rare antiques, and an old map served as the most dramatic and visible artwork. In part, this was a blessing. Because the apartment was so small we did not want to overwhelm it with drama. But the place not only functioned well, it was truly a pleasurable room to be in. It served as our calling card to New York, and its publication in design magazines helped attract many new clients. In fact, the room's beautiful monochromatic color scheme became something of our signature and was much imitated in the years that followed.

The room's existing fireplace, opposite and above, provided inspiration. The desk is covered in American homespun. Two draped tables on either side of the bed, right, hide storage. All other furniture is movable, small in scale, and multifunctional.

This elegantly proportioned main room serves as living room,
dining room, and reading room. The site of much
entertaining, it is as comfortable for a crowd of fifty
as when the owner is alone.

AN URBAN LIVING/DINING ROOM

The problems in designing the living room for a New York single woman were less severe—her apartment consisted of two floors of a brownstone on Manhattan's Upper East Side—but no less complex. This elegantly proportioned main room, 24 by 24 feet, had to serve as living room, dining room, and reading room. It was also to be the site of much entertaining and had to be as comfortable for a crowd of fifty as it was for its owner when she was alone.

Our first decision was to create an open space, with furniture grouped along the wall, which made the room seem even larger. We wanted cozy seating areas that could accommodate up to six people, so we used chairs that could be pulled up to any spot, rather than filling the room with heavy, bulky sofas. Instead, we designed banquettes for each side of the entrance archway, which we raised nearly to the ceiling to emphasize the height of the room. Pictures were hung in a double stack for the same reason.

Because the room received good afternoon light, we kept the window coverings sheer and hung a large mirror to expand the light and reflect the room, increasing the sense of vitality. We also placed a comfortable reclining chair and ottoman near the window to take advantage of the light.

Again we used a monochromatic color scheme, but this time in cool blues and pale grays. The client had requested "an apartment in the sky," and the colors evoked that feeling. We used dark wood to add impact, and against the pale background the furniture stands out like pieces of sculpture. All the pieces have an airy feeling and are light

enough to be easily moved. The sleek and modern feel of the room is offset by Pierre Charreau wicker chairs and an Arts and Crafts ratchet chair that reclines. Instead of a simple dining table, we chose a square English Sheraton table that also serves as a library table, and whose leaves—which can

Banquettes hug the wall to leave the flow of space unimpeded. Opposite: The dining table's beautifully figured leaves hang on the wall as a kind of minimal artwork.

expand the table so that it seats sixteen—are so beautifully detailed that we hung them on the wall like paintings.

Adding to the light feeling is a raffia rug from the South of France and an airy wire candle chandelier that hangs high overhead. The finished result is functional and restrained yet lyrical, not unlike a ballet set, and perfect for a single woman in the city.

A ROOM FOR ENTERTAINING

The grand room we created for entertaining in a large residence in Aspen could not have been more different from the other two. This room, in a huge modernist house, needed to serve only one purpose, entertaining. But the vast room, 30 by 50 feet with 24-foot ceilings, had to be comfortable for any number of people, from an intimate group of four to a vivacious party of a hundred. We also wanted to warm up the hard concrete walls and slate floor.

Our first decision was to establish three distinct seating areas, each of which could comfortably seat eight. One was grouped around the piano, and the second faced the room's large fireplace, a natural focal point. To create a third, we placed a center table at one end that could also be used to serve drinks and hors d'oeuvres.

Surprisingly for such a modern room, our inspiration was paintings by Vermeer. We wanted to create a vaguely seventeenth-century feel to offset the starkness of the room. We used large-scale furniture to bring drama to the space—anything too small would simply be dwarfed—and leathers, suedes, velvets, and chenilles to give the room tactile warmth. The dark wood pieces are French Regency, Jacobean, and French Gothick, with built-in banquettes and 1940s French leather club chairs used throughout, to provide familiar and comfortable elements. Mirrors are framed in ebony woods, and Dutch chandeliers add interest to the high ceilings. Strong patterns in the upholstery fabrics focus the eye within the large space, and the sparkle of mirrors and silver offsets the gray tones of the space. Heavy serge curtains at the windows are scaled to the space but are quite soft to the touch.

Despite its size, the room functions well on a day-to-day basis and is never overwhelming. At night it glows and is strangely inviting. It draws you in, which may be the ultimate success for a room whose purpose is to provide a beautiful background for spending time with family and friends.

Overscaled objects in the entry, including a huge Italian Baroque mirror, are used to stand up to the concrete floors and walls of a large Aspen house.

Inspired by the paintings of Vermeer, we sought to create a vaguely seventeenth—century feel to offset the starkness of this grand room for entertaining.

Seating areas, above, add coziness to the hall. In a guest room, left, walls are paneled on the horizontal to draw the eye down.

Large-scale furniture on a French Gothic rug, opposite, brings drama to the vast space. Leathers, suedes, velvets, and chenilles give the room tactile warmth in a cold climate. The chandelier and mirror are Dutch.

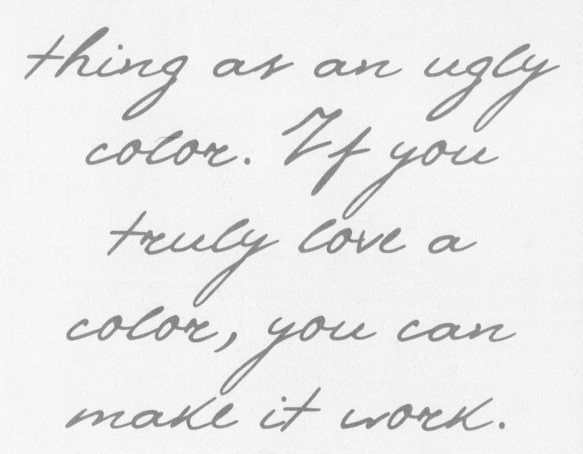

There is no such thing as an ugly color. If you truly love a color, you can make it work.

chapter five
Color

Nothing changes a room more dramatically than color. There is no better way to enliven a space than painting it, no quicker way to add punch to a room than bringing in items of vivid, contrasting color. Nothing is more restfully beautiful than a room in a subtle range of shades of a single color, and nothing can destroy a sense of harmony more quickly than jarring, discordant hues.

Color is powerful, and it is complicated. Whole courses are taught on the subject of color theory in art schools, and one of the highest compliments you can pay a painter, fashion designer, or decorator is to call him or her a brilliant colorist. But you don't need to be a genius or an artist to work with color successfully. Though the subject can be intimidating, understanding a few basic principles will ensure that you can use color effectively.

The first rule is: There is no such thing as an ugly color. Any color can come alive and be made to work wonderfully when it is put with compatible ones. Even the muddiest brown can be glorious when paired with the right blues and white. Some of the most chic schemes involve shades of brown, gray, or dark greens, paired with wonderful complementary colors. If you truly love a color, you can make it work.

But when you are first experimenting with color, don't go overboard and don't spend a lot of money on vividly colored items you may later regret. Start with bold color in an area rug or on canvas slipcovers. A coat of paint involves more time than money, and walls can be repainted fairly easily if you make a dreadful mistake. The more you understand about color before you begin, the happier you will be with the results.

Color is entirely dependent on light. The more the light varies, the more a color will change. Grays can become blues, turquoise can turn to gray, even green can

Colors should

harmonize but

In a bedroom in our country house, the walls
are painted an unusual green. The high-gloss
paint creates an atmospheric effect.

they don't need

to match.

appear gray under certain lighting conditions. Color changes as light changes, and natural light is never static. Light varies according to the time of day, the weather, the geographic properties of the landscape—light at the beach is far different from in the mountains, for example. Winter light is cooler than summer light, and nothing reflects more light than snow, which acts as a prism, scattering light in all directions. Light in the country is affected by the green of grass and trees, while urban light tends to be more cool and gray. The light of Paris is gray, and in the South of France it is yellow. Manhattan has a blue light, while the sunlight of the Midwest is harsh white.

Even indoors, light can vary enormously. The amount of sunlight admitted by windows, the texture of surfaces—from matte to shiny to mirror finishes—even the amount and kind of artificial light will change the way color appears. So it is important to study the light in your home, to know which rooms get the most or the least light, the most pleasant time of day in each room, the range of light—how dark it is on a winter afternoon compared to a sunny summer day.

With active light, even plain white walls become like a movie screen, registering subtle shifts projected by the constantly changing light. North light, or frontal light from a single source, which is uniformly diffuse and indirect, can result in flat and shadowless space. The light preferred by painters does not automatically make a space feel good to be in and can be bland and affectless.

Paint is a way to control the visual temperature of a room. White feels cool in summer, but even whites can range in effect from warm custard to cool violet. Complementary colors subdue one another when mixed but, conversely, intensify one another when juxtaposed. Green is a diplomatic color, in the middle of the spectrum, cool enough to feel sheltering and warm enough to work with dark woods. Beige, a mixture of red and green, is simultaneously warm and cool.

But the eye doesn't like too much uniformity, because then it has nowhere to go for a rest (which is why fluorescent light is unpleasant). The eye seeks out contrasts and will inevitably go to the point of greatest contrast. This is why using warm and cool polarities will energize a room. On the other hand, forcing the eye to keep readjusting from light to dark can be exhausting.

A room is much more pleasant to be in if it relates to the exterior light. This is why color schemes for urban apartments are usually more subtle—silvery blues and grays, pales beiges and creams. In a more natural or vibrant setting, colors should be bright, since the transition from outdoors to inside will be less abrupt. Think of the color on a wall as being mixed with the color of

In a monochromatic room, the challenge is to make certain that the limited range of colors does not become boring.

The living room of our country house is largely done in shades of whites and off-whites. But the varied textures of the walls, ceiling, and floors add richness and a variety of light effects. Against the pale background, furniture pieces stand out like sculptures.

the light hitting it, and adjust your color choice accordingly. If you want to use a lot of different colors in one room, make sure they are all of equal intensity.

Colors close in hue and value—ones that fall in roughly the same place on the scale of light and dark—can create a sort of atmospheric shimmer and can unify disparate elements. On the other hand, painting each room a different shade creates the sensation of a larger house, since each space feels different. But keep in mind the views from room to room when choosing colors and complementary hues. If they are harmonious, they will enhance the visual flow of space.

When color is integral to the material—stone, wood, metal—it registers less strongly. Using wood is a way to have the effect of color without its being perceived as color. Wood evokes warmth while absorbing light, and even dark wood can appear luminous. Focusing on texture and sheen is a way to accentuate the available light or overcome a gray light that lacks color and luminosity. Reflective surfaces—mirror, silver, chrome, shiny fabrics, dark polished woods—all compound the effect and magnify the light.

All this information can be overwhelming. But much of what's important to know about color is actually instinctual. It is much more important to look than to think when it comes to color. Always look at swatches

of paint or samples of color in the actual room where you are planning to use them, and under as many different light situations as possible. Note the way colors change from daylight to night, on a sunny or a cloudy day, in the morning and afternoon, and under artificial light, before making your final decisions.

Most important, always use colors you like, and never choose colors because they are "in style." Fashion changes and you will soon grow tired of colors you don't love.

Colors should harmonize; they don't need to match. A room is enriched by variations of a color, a blend of two colors, by the use of complementary colors rather than similar shades. If a room contains too much of a single color, if the pieces are too "matchy-matchy," the color loses its impact and we stop seeing it—no matter how strong, the color will be reduced to a neutral. Offbeat and unexpected color combinations and contrasts, however, never lose their punch. One of our favorites, for example, is olive with cinnamon.

When using difficult colors, recognize that it is risky. That doesn't mean it is impossible or that you should not attempt it. But if you rarely see certain colors used, it is for a reason. Plan carefully and accordingly when using these colors. Mellow colors are much easier to work and live with, although in the

In a Miami house, warm golden walls and bold French furniture of the 1940s stand up to the intense light.

A suite of French furniture from the
1940s in the dining room. Opposite:
In the library, a rendering of a stage
set adds vivid color.

right setting a shock of color can be invaluable. But keep in mind that dark colors on walls only look good in a shiny, gloss finish or when glazed. And when working with hard or unusual colors such as reds, rusts, browns, or yellows it is always better to use those with a grayed tone. When choosing a shade of a color like chrome yellow, always select the value that is more gray. Grayer values of a color are far easier to live with and work with than clear, sharp tones.

Now, with electric light, our color sensibility has shifted. We tend to prefer a more muted, fresher approach. Today, color values have to reflect well in electric light, which, far more than natural light or candlelight, is the standard by which we judge colors now.

Fortunately, we have largely abandoned the concept that colors are room-specific, that certain colors can only be used in a bedroom, for example, or that a bedroom

Color is powerful and it is complicated.

The current vogue in decorating is for pale, washed-out colors. While we were among the pioneers of this look, we have become much bolder and more experimental in our use of color. Rich wall color can add dimension to your possessions and can stand up to strong pieces.

In the early seventeenth and eighteenth centuries vivid colors were all the rage in decoration. Pigment was hard to obtain and exceedingly expensive, so color was a luxury item, and one that the wealthy indulged in exuberantly. It was a period of extravagant and brilliant color—rich and pungent blues and purples, scarlets and other reds. Rich colors set off the extravagant gilded furniture and the strong lines of the best furniture of the period. And both gilding and rich color looked especially beautiful in candlelight.

needs to be pale in order to be restful, or that a library can only be painted in dark colors. We have created a lovely library all in white lacquer—where the books provide the only color. We have lacquered a bedroom charcoal gray with great success. What is most important is how the colors look and work in a room. That, and that alone, should determine what is appropriate.

In general, most of our successful projects fall into one of three categories. It is helpful to use color in one of these three ways when decorating a room.

The first is monochromatic. This is the easiest and works especially well in city apartments, which is why we followed this

The rich browns of the wood floors, doors, and furniture predominate. These are offset by the white walls and touches of blue-gray upholstery.

Lemon-yellow walls and a set
of Rhulmann chairs covered in
magenta velvet create a spirited
environment for dining and
contrast with the white walls of
the other rooms, inset.

*When it comes to color,
it is much more
important to look
than to think.*

approach in both of our Manhattan apartments. The first was done completely in golden beiges; the current one features pale grayed greens, giving an overall shimmering and almost evanescent effect.

With this approach, all the colors fall within a small range, from walls to upholstery fabrics to smaller decorative elements. It is not important what the primary color is—it can be taupe, brown, or parchment, pale silvery blue, even a warm pink or coral. But all the shades must coordinate throughout the room, with no jarring elements. Also, limiting the range of color precludes the mistake that many people make of using too many colors—especially too many small bits of color—so that a room ends up looking like an Easter egg hunt or a color chart.

With the monochromatic approach the challenge is to make certain that the limited range of colors does not become boring. This is done by varying the intensity of the shades and by using a variety of rich textures. Adding a bit of contrast is key.

•

The second approach is to use white as the predominant color with shots of bright color. This is especially successful in a house we decorated in Southampton, where all the walls and paneling are a glossy white and most of the large upholstered pieces, and even the rug, are white. This white backdrop is animated with a bright yellow leather wing chair, deep red

fabrics on side chairs and pillows, and the dark brown of a daybed, the floors, and several wood furniture pieces.

This approach works best in rooms with good architectural detailing and high-quality furniture. White can be unforgiving, and awkwardly proportioned rooms, or those lacking in detailing, can actually look worse. And because pieces of furniture stand out against white, almost like sculptures in a gallery, they need to be of a quality and scale commensurate with the attention they will receive. But when working with the best spaces and objects, this approach can yield results that are dramatic, beautiful, and supremely comfortable.

•

The third approach we occasionally use is to indulge in strong colors. This is probably the trickiest of all, but it can be effective—and inexpensive, since paint becomes a primary resource. We chose this approach when decorating a downtown Manhattan apartment for a magazine editor. Here we used color to compensate for a lack of architecture, and for a limited budget. When she was single, this editor did not own grand pieces, nor did she want a formal apartment. She wanted a living space that reflected her youth, energy, and creativity. This quirky space was not where she planned to live forever, and she gave us the chance to experiment and have fun. We decided to use colors inspired by Matisse's

In a country house in Southampton, the paneling is glossy white, but a chrome-yellow wing chair and a drawing by Richard Serra become strong focal points.

White with splashes of color works best in rooms with good architectural detailing.

paintings of interiors. We painted the low ceilings to provide a focal point, and there is actually more color on the ceiling than on the walls. All of the shapes become volumes of color themselves, and it is the color that one notices first, rather than the space or the objects within it.

Furniture pieces were chosen for their forms and strong personality, and were mixed with items that had belonged to the client's parents and that she had loved while growing up. A pair of old armchairs was upholstered in purple; new ladderback chairs around the dining table were painted blue. The neutral upholstered pieces were played off of colorful, funky pieces. A big, vividly colored kilim-upholstered ottoman served as both a coffee table and as extra seating when entertaining.

Needless to say, when using these kinds of strong colors—reds, greens, and purples—you need to know what you are doing, putting them together almost as if you were painting a picture.

Forget rules. The only important consideration is how the colors look and work in a room.

Inspired by the paintings of Matisse, we used vivid colors throughout this downtown apartment, especially on the ceilings, and furniture with clean graphic lines. The X table next to the bed, inset, is by Dwellings.

The most important consideration for any piece of furniture is suitability.

chapter six

Furniture

Furniture is the most conspicuous element of any room, the most crucial to the way it functions and looks, and will probably take up a greater percentage of your budget than any other aspect of decorating. The more you understand about furniture, how it works, what pieces you need, and the history of furniture styles, the more likely you are to avoid expensive mistakes and to end up with a harmonious array of pieces that fulfill all your needs.

The most important consideration for any piece of furniture is suitability. Does it perform its function efficiently and beautifully? This standard applies for everything from a simple stool to an antique sideboard. Will you use the piece? Do you have proper space for it? Is it harmonious with the other furnishings in the room?

Putting together a room full of furniture is essentially creating a visual composition—it requires pictorial balance. This is why it's so important to create a floor plan.

Never approach the placement of furniture piecemeal. And remember, furniture can be made as prominent or as subdued as you like. In a white room, furniture in dark woods or upholstered in dark fabrics will stand out like sculptures within the space. Or you can opt to make furniture blend in with the background through the use of monochromatic fabrics, pale matching woods, and subtle, simple shapes.

Scale is also crucial. Consider the proportions and forms of furniture. Is a piece light and frivolous or heavy and visually weighted? Heavy pieces will not work with tables poised on thin spindly legs, for example, and a low sofa will not work in a room full of tall furniture. Curved pieces work best with other pieces that echo the curves in some way. Too many dainty objects get lost in a large space. But a small room doesn't necessarily require small pieces. In some cases, it's best to use fewer, larger pieces to visually enlarge a small space.

To put together a roomful

In a gentleman's Manhattan apartment, opposite and above, that is flooded with light, wood furniture from various periods adds up to a harmony in brown. The mahogany armchairs are French, the drum table is Indonesian. A strié effect on the walls adds depth.

of furniture is to create a visual composition.

Even when using furniture entirely of a single period or style, it is necessary to keep in mind the compatibility of form and shapes. Within one period there can be vast differences in proportion and styling. You must create a rhythm of proportions and functions. And it is important not to create a time capsule, or a museumlike period room. The room must still function for today and clearly be a product of modern times.

Putting together a harmonious and pleasing arrangement is not simply a matter of matching periods or even continents or countries of origin. You need to understand the spirit and intention of the designers and craftsmen who originally created the pieces.

In a city bedroom an American
Sheraton bed, an English side
table, and a Viennese cabinet.
Opposite: An American twig-and-
plywood chair, an African ladder,
and an American nineteenth-
century chest all contribute to
a unity of mood.

Symmetry is desirable, but it can be achieved through weight and balance. You don't always need a pair.

A suite of 1940s French furniture in a Miami house, opposite, is placed in an asymmetrical arrangement. In the bedroom, above, a Belgian leather screen and a 1920s English steel bench. The writing table, right, is French, from the 1940s, and was inspired by a seventeenth-century Spanish original. The chair is Italian.

Furniture doesn't have to match. Most of us grew up seeing advertisements for dining room sets with matching sideboards, living rooms with matching coffee and end tables, bedroom "suites" with coordinating dressers and vanities. This kind of uniformity can be death to creativity and unnecessarily limits your options. Never be afraid to mix pieces of various periods and styles, as long as you keep a few principles in mind. Unity can be achieved through the colors of the woods or through a similarity of spirit or form. A room is much stronger and more personal if it doesn't have "sets" of matching chairs, dressers, and so on. Not even bedside tables or lamps have to match. While symmetry may be desirable, it can almost always be achieved through weight and balance. As a general rule, you don't need a pair.

Even in an elaborate room, not all pieces should be grand. A simple pine table can be useful and appropriate, and it can be enhanced by being painted or draped with a rug, tapestry, or tablecloth. But it is important to keep a balance. The majority of pieces in a room should be of approximately equal value—you don't want to insult a beautiful, valuable piece of furniture with a cheap upstart. This doesn't mean you can't add wit to a room with an unusual chair or stool, an unexpected accessory, or a small decorative piece. But generally, all the major pieces should be in harmony in

regard to value as well as weight. And objects don't necessarily have to be used as they were intended. You can put a small table on a larger table, for instance, to showcase it like a piece of sculpture.

With less expensive furniture, authenticity is the key. A small old rusted metal garden table in a grand room can add charm, but not if it is striped and gilded. Furniture should

never pretend to be what it isn't. Don't try to fill gaps in a room with mediocre pieces. It is better to have bare space than ugly or uncomfortable pieces. When your budget is less than ideal, concentrate on acquiring simple, honest pieces. Opt for good strong shapes, sturdy and functional design, and classic proportions. A wonderful pine gate-leg table is useful in many situations. A reproduction English pedestal table with good proportions can be used in many different rooms and will never be a bad investment.

Don't be impressed with labels, provenance, or price—look at the objects themselves. Perhaps the most important thing in dealing with furniture is to understand which styles and periods work together—and which don't. You can educate your eye through books on furniture history and the decorative arts, studying period rooms in museums, and looking at successful rooms in decorating books and magazines. After putting together hundreds of rooms, we have developed guidelines about grouping furniture that may prove helpful.

Simple modern pieces, such as a clean geometric Parsons table, work with nearly every period, in virtually any room. A classical Roman daybed is not very different in its form, shape, or intentions from a Mies van der Rohe daybed. Antique Chinese furniture is modern in its lines and therefore works beautifully even in a room otherwise full of modern pieces.

A Biedermeier daybed or chair won't work with a seventeenth-century Italian chair. A Renaissance piece probably won't work with a nineteenth-century Romantic piece. And don't assume that if they share a country of origin, pieces from different eras

will be compatible. An American Chippendale or gilded American Empire chest of drawers won't work with a severe Arts and Crafts table. It is far more important for the spirit of the pieces to be in accord than for them to share their place of manufacture. For example, an English neo-Gothic piece will probably work well with American Arts and Crafts, whereas English Regency furniture, although made at virtually the same time, probably will not.

In a large living room with a fireplace, you will undoubtedly want a sofa, a large side table, and a lamp, for what could be better than reading by the fire? But if a room is very large, it is probably best to break up the space with groupings of furniture, which bring a vast space down to a more inviting scale. Furniture groupings allow for a variety of uses, especially when entertaining.

We have learned through the years that when trying to find pieces for strictly utilitarian purposes, anything from holding a stereo or TV to housing equipment for a home office, it is better to use modern, manufactured pieces, or have pieces specially made, rather than looking for an antique that will serve the purpose. This is usually best in the case of bedside tables with drawers; tiered shelving and étagères, especially for the bathroom; desks; free-

English botanical prints hang above an Irish Georgian console, with an American painted box beneath. The urn is Roman, from the second century A.D.

standing bookshelves; home office equipment and computer stations; and television stands. It is simply too difficult to find old pieces to be adapted, and too often the reconfigured pieces look a little silly.

While a decorator can give you access to unusual pieces, antiques, and to-the-trade showrooms, sources that would be unavailable to you otherwise, the rise of chain stores, moderate-price catalogs, and shopping on the Internet has made it easier than ever to find good design at reasonable prices. However, because these stores and

UPHOLSTERY

For many people, upholstered furniture is the most difficult purchase they face in furnishing a home. With the variety of styles, quality, prices, and sizes—not to mention thousands of fabric choices—on the market, it's not surprising that selecting a sofa or chair can be an ordeal. The first rule to remember is that this is a major purchase, and you should always buy the best upholstery you can afford. Nowhere is that old adage "Buy cheap, buy twice" more applicable. High-quality pieces are expensive

If your upholstered pieces are in classic shapes, you will never grow bored with them.

manufacturers have to reach a mass audience, they often create pieces to correspond to popular taste. Be wary of pieces that exaggerate the style of the moment or enlarge or change the scale. Ironically, we have found that the items that don't sell in these chain stores, those that are marked down or closed out, often have the most classic and restrained design. Never hesitate to avail yourself of these items. Just because a piece is a bargain doesn't mean it isn't beautiful and useful. The opposite also holds true. It is easy to spend a lot of money on ugly and inappropriate furniture.

In a Park Avenue living room, French Empire, Directoire, and Consulate furniture. The chandelier is Irish Waterford crystal.

but they will last a lifetime. They can be slipcovered or reupholstered, and if they are a classic shape, you will never grow bored with them. A good sofa can always be reused, moved to a different room, or even passed on to children or friends. Cheap upholstered pieces rarely last longer than a few years and are usually not comfortable even during their brief lifetimes.

But because upholstered pieces are expensive, people fall prey to the idea that they should be the standouts in a room. This is a major mistake. Sofas and upholstered chairs should never be the focal point of a room. Upholstered pieces should function and be comfortable above all, but visually they should recede into the back-

In a home in Bethesda, Maryland, comfort mixes with grandeur in a den. The golden tones of the room were inspired by the Art Nouveau poster. Fortuny fabrics designed at the same period are used on the overscaled sofa and ottoman and for the curtains. The club chair is covered in velvet corduroy.

Even in an elaborate room, not all pieces should be grand.

Top: In the entry, an English breakfront is flanked by a pair of Italian painted chairs. Right: The library of the same apartment is paneled in mellow oak to create a backdrop for Impressionist paintings. The étagère is Directoire, the brackets are Regency. The pair of chairs, opposite, is Consulate.

ground. These pieces should provide the backbone of a room, not overwhelm it. An oversized upholstered piece fills a room badly and reduces the flexibility of the space. We prefer smaller-scale pieces, which allow for greater visual variety in a room and maximum flexibility.

A standard long sofa is usually not necessary. A sofa, no matter how long, is rarely used by more than two people at once. This holds true even at crowded parties. So in most cases it makes more sense to have a few smaller pieces rather than one big one. Perhaps a loveseat will serve as well as a larger, bulkier sofa. Small, armless slipper chairs are great additional seating—elegant, comfortable, and easily moved, even during a party. They are great space savers and can be placed out of the way when not needed.

When thinking about buying a sofa, keep in mind its scale, shape, and volume. For example, a skirt on a sofa will ground the piece, adding to its sense of volume and weight. But in a room that needs air and light, particularly in a small room, a sofa that is raised up on feet of two or three inches may be preferable.

A tufted back is appropriate for certain styles but generally does not work in a modern room, whereas a sofa with a low back and low arms is universally appropriate. Square-shaped pieces generally don't work in a country room and are more appropriate for stylized, urban interiors.

Always sit in a sofa or chair first to test the feel. Make certain that the seat is not so deep that your back won't rest comfortably and that your legs can bend naturally. Test the arms to see if they fall at a comfortable height and are conducive to long, relaxing sits. Many very sculptural or cubistic pieces, even some considered masterpieces of modernism, were simply not designed to accommodate the human body comfortably for long periods of time.

We also want to dispel the myth of the down sofa. Many people believe that because they are more expensive, down sofas are the best choice. A sofa whose cushions are stuffed only with down is neither comfortable nor practical. Cushions of solid foam will not last forever, however. By far the best choice is upholstery in which the loose cushions are made of a core of foam or Dacron batting that is surrounded by down. This still provides softness but has much greater structure and therefore comfort. The cushions are lighter and more flexible than ones stuffed with pure down and won't slide around and lose their shape the way down cushions do.

Upholstery fabrics need to be heavy and sturdy enough to withstand their intended use, but not so heavy that they are uncomfortable or hot or rough to the touch, such as heavy tweeds or wools. The subject of fabrics is discussed in greater detail in chapter seven.

SEVEN SOFAS

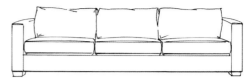

There are seven basic styles of sofa that work best. We have used these over and over again, in endless permutations, and one of them is appropriate for virtually any decorating scheme.

Probably the simplest, and the easiest to adapt to any room, is the low, armless sofa we designed for our country house. With its single long seat cushion, raised on small wood legs, and loose back pillows, it is comfortable and unobtrusive, perfect for crowds (its lack of arms means more people can sit on it at once than on a standard sofa), and it can even be used as a guest bed in a pinch. It is amazingly versatile and works in the most minimal or most elaborate of rooms, depending on the fabric in which it is upholstered.

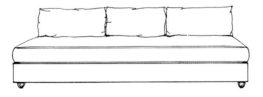

A more structured and therefore imposing sofa is the one we designed for a Southampton home, inspired by a classic piece from the 1950s by the great Texas designer William Pahlman. Its squared-off arms and cushions give it a geometric presence, so it works extremely well in contemporary or even stark settings. We covered it in a white hopsack and placed it in a white grid-paneled room. But in a softer material, such as silk velvet, it would also work very well in a traditional room. Best of all, it is extremely comfortable for curling up in and reading.

Perhaps the most basic, and thus universally appropriate, sofa we have designed is the Dwellings "Classic" sofa that we used

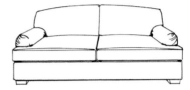

in our own Manhattan apartment. With its gentle curved back, low curved arms, and short foursquare legs, it is subdued yet elegant. Its fitted seat cushions ensure a clean appearance at all times and make this the perfect background sofa for almost any style or period of decor.

More playful is the sofa in one fashion executive's Manhattan apartment. With its tufted back, it evokes a grandeur that is underscored by its swooping curved arms and its high turned and gilded legs (not to mention the vivid color of velvet that we

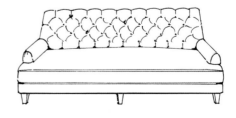

used for her apartment). The sofa is capacious and comfortable but not massive and is deliberately designed to hold its own in an eclectic setting.

Also tufted is the banquette in our Manhattan apartment. A banquette, which can be made to any length to fit specific areas, is often ideal when there is another sofa in the room. Ours, with its tufting on seat and

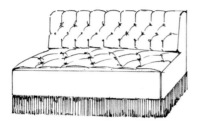

back, simple geometric shape, high back, and hem of fringe, is evocative of the nineteenth century but was designed to work with the room's more modern furniture.

The sofa in a grand Fifth Avenue apartment, with the gentle swooping curve of its stylized camel back, skirt with passementerie trimming, and curved arms, is

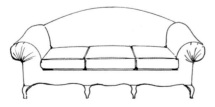

ideal for more elegant rooms with a high degree of finish, used for formal functions.

A more fanciful and curvy piece is the sofa we designed for a playful, feminine

apartment. The back, arms, and even the base and feet curve, as if the sofa were dancing. This sofa is more limited than the others and is suited only to fanciful interiors, especially rooms evoking the decorative arts of the 1930s or '40s.

MIXING IT UP

Always remember that there are wonderful alternatives to sofas and chairs to provide seating. Consider recamiers or daybeds, banquettes, small stools, or a large ottoman that can serve as seating or, with the addition of a tray, as a coffee table. These pieces add versatility as well as visual variety. And while an antique sofa, settee, or chaise may not be suitable as the foundation of a room, it can provide a pleasing contrast to more substantial upholstered pieces. Even in a modern room, something beautiful from the past, or even a reproduction, will add warmth and charm.

Pieces need not be grand or weighty or impressive to be worthy of consideration. Charm is created by a sense of the temporary and the surprising. It is often through

Seating is provided by a Directoire daybed next to the fireplace. The mirror reflects a Picasso tapestry.

small touches such as rugs, pillows, unexpected colors, or decorative items that a room comes to life.

These general principles will help you in selecting the right furniture, but they are just that, guidelines. Any piece of furniture you love, whatever its provenance or value, should be proudly displayed and used. It is your commitment to an object that will make it work in a room. The only hard and fast rule is not to take your rooms too seriously. Feel free to experiment, try different things, break rules that you have been taught are inviolable. This will not only help develop your eye, it is great fun and will reward you with rooms that function efficiently and that you will truly love.

Any piece of furniture you love should be proudly displayed and used.

In the library of our house, a German eighteenth-century Louis XVI desk is accented with a pair of Sèvres bisque porcelain caryatid lamps, opposite. The small writing table is by the French cabinet-maker Carabar, the mahogany chair is Directoire. An English fireman's ladder from the nineteenth century is used to reach the shelves. In the living room, above, the daybed is Directoire.

In our guest cottage, a French upholstered
screen serves as a backdrop for a nineteenth-
century sofa and an eighteenth-century
neoclassical Italian chair. Opposite: In a bedroom of the main house, a French *bureau plat*
contrasts with a Mexican chest of drawers
inlaid with bone.

In our Manhattan apartment, a steel daybed, opposite, is used as a sofa. Painted Italian cabinets from the eighteenth century hold globes and obelisks.

It is often through small touches, such as rugs, pillows, unexpected colors, or decorative items, that a room comes to life.

Walls, floors, and ceilings are underestimated when it comes to the impact they can have.

chapter seven
Surfaces

The walls, floors, and ceilings are the largest surfaces in any rooms, yet they are too often underestimated when it comes to the impact—positive or negative—they can have.

FLOORS AND RUGS

The floor is the foundation of any room. It should act as both a decorative feature and the anchor for all the other elements in the room. The floor gives a face to a room, whether covered in wood planks or parquet, stone, tile, carpet, or any of a wide variety of unusual materials—including synthetics, cork, linoleum, bamboo, even polished concrete. Floors darken or lighten the atmosphere, bring reflective shine, or demarcate spaces. Floors bring pattern and texture to a room or help disguise awkward proportions. Stripes, for example, either subtle or bold, painted or stained on a floor or brought in via carpeting, can widen a long, narrow room.

Nothing warms up a room like a beautiful rug. A rug provides a visual footprint, a guide to how to use the space within a room. Rugs can draw people to a seating area, for example, or indicate a pathway to another space. They are a means of not only adding warmth but bringing coherence to a space, to differentiate path from place.

It is generally best to use the simplest rug possible. If you have a gorgeous antique rug, by all means use it, but these rugs are not necessary. In fact, rugs with central medallions are the hardest to use in a room because they limit furniture placement. These rugs were made for perfectly proportioned rooms, the kind that are common in France, for example, but that rarely exist in this country. So unless they fit beautifully within your room, be wary of these rugs. Oriental rugs can be glorious, but they can also be difficult to work with, since most are predominantly red and blue, and these colors don't often lend themselves to

The entry of a midwestern house has antique optical-illusion flooring and a pair of eighteenth-century German consoles topped by English mirrors from the 1940s.

The floors are
the foundation

The delicacy of an antique
Indian paisley on an Italian
painted chair contrasts with
a rough cobblestone floor.

# of any room.

modern schemes. Large-scale, formal Orientals ultimately work well only with classic American or English furniture.

In the early part of the twentieth century people chose rugs that filled the room, but today we prefer smaller rugs that reveal the wood or stone floors beneath. If you have beautiful floors, why cover them up completely? Usually the best solution is to use smaller rugs that demarcate specific seating areas or hallways, while heightening awareness of the floor beneath.

People obsess about finding the "perfect" rug and feel that a room can never work until the rug is in place. But in fact, we have never found a rug before creating a plan or color scheme. Nor have we ever built a room around a rug or carpet. Many people feel that if they design a room first, they will never find a rug that "goes with" it. This is a groundless fear. There is an enormous array of carpets of all sizes, colorings, and patterns available today—both antique and modern—and a room's design should never be inhibited by worries about finding some elusive masterpiece of a rug. People attach far too much importance to a rug. A rug should not drive the design of a room but serve as a backdrop.

If you don't have or can't afford a beautiful rug, sisal or seagrass, or any woven wool in a pale subtle color, provides a neutral backdrop and is usually the best solution. The ubiquity of sisal and seagrass over the past decade has made them fall from favor with trendsetters, but we still love these honest, natural materials. Their neutral colors and soothing, repetitive patterns make them ideal settings for furniture placement. They provide a kind of blank canvas on which to stage the drama of the room. And using them in adjoining rooms will pull together disparate spaces and give a sense of flow. We have used these inexpensive materials even in grand apartments to great effect. And though it is unfashionable at the moment, we also like the alternative of wall-to-wall carpeting, as long as it is a good-quality, low-cut pile or a tight loop or a subtle, small-scale pattern. Wall-to-wall carpeting can smooth out the imperfections of a room or help unify a complicated layout. It is especially warming in a bedroom.

Carpeting will visually expand a space. The choice of carpeting sets the tone. A darker rug, for example, will suggest a more formal interior, while a paler, driftwood-colored rug works best with more casual furnishings. Usually it is best to create a floor palette that is soothing rather than jarring or immediately eye-catching. In unusual spaces, such as a small foyer or a powder room, it may be appropriate to create a dramatic floor of patterned wood or tile. But in general the floor should not act as the focal point; rather, it should be a strong yet quiet foundation for all else that happens in that space.

WALLS

Walls can enrich a room quietly but immeasurably. Indeed, our firm first became known for our attention to walls, with elaborate finishes and rich textures created with stencils, strié effects, glazes, layerings of colors, and decorative finishes. Unusual materials—sheets of wood veneer or parchment, for example—will enliven a room and engage the eye without detracting from the artworks and furniture within.

Wood-paneled walls are beautiful, whether modern or antique, but even these can be enriched through wire brushing and liming them, or by staining them beautiful rich colors. But staining properly is critical. It is important to achieve the right tones and depth of color, so that the paneling doesn't appear flat or one-dimensional.

There are many ways besides painting to treat a wall. Often a richer effect can be achieved by making the color integral to the plaster itself. Combing wet plaster with brooms, for example, to gently groove the walls gives a subtle textured stripe effect.

Even Sheetrock, the bane of any new construction or renovation, can be treated to enrich its flatness by using pigmented plaster or by treating the walls with plaster compound or drywall compound. Sheetrock walls look wonderful when painted with high-gloss paint, which gives them a subtle reflective quality. This is best done in pale or very dark colors. Even rooms painted in white high-gloss paint, which was once taboo, can yield lovely, light-enhancing results.

Walls can also be covered with fabric to great effect, to add texture and pattern, though we do not like fabric that is quilted or otherwise upholstered. If there is an acoustical problem in a room, we will pad fabric walls with felt, but we actually prefer paper-backed fabric applied to the walls. Upholstery fabrics on the wall can be highly effective. Striped fabrics will give height to a room with low ceilings. And heavily textured linen can add richness to any room. There is nothing lovelier than walls covered in linen and then painted a beautiful color, as if they were an artist's canvas. But beware of using nubby silk on walls, as the natural imperfections of the silk can catch the light in an ugly way and draw attention to its flaws.

Another economical way to add texture is to apply inexpensive embossed wallpaper and then paint over it with high-gloss paint. The resulting, almost subliminal, pattern subtly enriches the room without drawing attention to itself. And because a repeated pattern on walls visually expands a room, it is especially effective in small spaces.

Almost every wall surface offers possibilities for enriching a space. Bathroom walls can be covered with sheets of milk glass, for example, or sheets of glass painted with colors on the back to add a practical, yet richly reflective, finish to the room.

Among the many wall treatments we favor are, clockwise from right: walls covered in a printed fabric; hand-stenciling, in this case in a Turkish motif that is found elsewhere in this dining room; painting paneling different shades of flat and high-gloss white, to add a subtle shimmering effect to a room; and, center, contrasting dyed plaster walls with opaque painted ones.

There are many ways besides painting to treat a wall.

In a midwestern bedroom, walls are covered with burlap stenciled in a pattern that echoes the motifs found in the English crewelwork curtains.

Almost every wall surface offers possibilities for enriching a space.

The subtle texture of
the stenciled canvas
walls of our Manhattan
apartment echoes the
tactile richness of the
shagreen daybed by
Jean-Michel Frank,
the Cy Twombly
painting, and the
Jean Arp sculpture.

Hand-painted stripes add
height and texture to a mid-
town Manhattan apartment.
Inset: Romantic stenciling in
a Connecticut country house.

visually expands a room.

And the effects don't need to be—nor should they be—dramatic. Subtle effects often wear the best over time and won't tire the eye or detract from the other elements in the room. This especially applies to stenciling. Stenciling was once something of a signature for our firm, and it remains a favorite way to deal with certain walls. Stenciling can pull together diverse architectural details or help camouflage bad, awkward proportions. In rooms that lack architectural detailing, for example, stenciling can create a sense of borders outlining a room. A stenciled border beneath a crown molding will add a sense of height by drawing the eye upward. And rich stenciling on walls can help substitute for a lack of art.

But stenciling works best when it is very subtle. We prefer it with an almost washed-out effect, as if it has been there for hundreds of years, a faded presence lending a kind of patina to a room. If a stencil is too strong or obvious it can be disastrous, looking too "crafted" and becoming a focal point rather than an enriching element of the scheme.

FABRICS

When choosing fabrics for upholstery, the most important consideration is their weight. Are the fabrics strong enough for their purpose? Certainly sheer fabrics can look lovely hanging as summer drapes at a window, but they would be a disaster on a sofa. And yes, dress fabrics may be dyed incredibly rich colors, but their density will not support the heavy use that furniture must handle, so they'll be far more effective used for small pillows. For upholstery, natural fibers in a high thread count are best—cottons, wools, mohairs, and blends. Thin chintzes may make fresh summer slipcovers but are too lightweight for upholstery. Rich silks will be too slippery for a living room chair and are best confined to a bedroom or used as drapes. And always remember to test a fabric against your bare skin. No one wants to sit on a fabric that is scratchy.

When selecting the fabrics for furniture or at the windows, stick to a limited color range, but vary the textures and patterns. Don't use the same fabric on all the pieces. That makes a room look too "matchy" and unnecessarily limits your options. Varied textures, even in a very limited color range, add both visual and tactile interest.

In general, select a range of color, tones, and textures you feel work well together. In fact, when we are drawing up a scheme for a client, we never begin by deciding which fabric will go where. We never pick, say, a sofa fabric first, and then choose other materials that will work with that. Instead, we select an array of fabrics that harmonize and only then decide where we are going to use each of them. We have never started with a patterned rug or a particular fabric and felt

A Middle Eastern carpet, an antique Turkish cloth, and a Russian chair create a harmony of curves.

In a Manhattan living room, the striped fabric on the walls was enriched by a hand-painted stripe of dull gold. The sofa is covered in a linen brocade; the pillows in silk velvets.

we had to work around that. That leads to results that are banal, "expected," and usually lifeless and dull.

Choose fabrics that are appropriate to the period of the furniture pieces on which they will be used. This doesn't mean that you must use only historically accurate fabrics but that the fabrics should be in the same spirit as the furniture. English chintzes, for example, will not work on period French chairs, which cry out for a silk damask or a solid. Bold dark wood Renaissance pieces would look silly upholstered in modern nubby fabrics. But this doesn't mean that grand and expensive pieces require grand and expensive fabrics. The power of simple materials cannot be overestimated. Even in grand rooms, the simplest materials often have the greatest impact.

It is often hard to visualize how a fabric will look based on the small samples supplied by a decorator or fabric house. Big patterns, especially, will look very different when you have twenty yards as opposed to a square foot. For this reason alone, be careful about using large-scale patterns on large pieces. Even solids will seem much more vivid on big pieces of furniture. This is why we seldom use these kinds of fabrics for sofas, for example, which we think should be nearly invisible within a room, like soft clouds of comfort. Bold, large patterns or vivid colors are best saved for small areas. Use these fabrics for pillows, on the seats of wood chairs, or on an ottoman, where they can add punch to a room but won't overwhelm the space. And if you love a very expensive fabric, don't despair. Buy a yard or two and use it for a pillow or seat back. You don't need a great deal of a fabric for it to add its impact to a room.

It is best to visualize the fabrics as creating color volumes, and then think about placing those volumes throughout the room. If there are two sofas and three chairs, think of how the color volumes—dark or light—will be balanced within the space, and how you want the room to read. Try to imagine the room as if you were creating a three-dimensional painting, juxtaposing one color shape against another, or composing a garden, with masses of flowers and foliage of varying shades and textures. A bit of vivid color or texture in a fabric can bring a whole composition to life. The rule that large pieces should be covered in neutrals should not limit the range of fabrics for small areas—in fact, quite the reverse. The ideal is not to have the fabrics match but to have them in tune, so that the space flows, the setting is serene and harmonious, but there are enough visual richness and surprises of tone, texture, and shape to keep the eye—and hand—consistently engaged and delighted.

In a Manhattan living room, a goldenrod sofa is played against lemon-yellow silk curtains. The fabric on the table is antique Indian crewelwork.

Imagine a room as if you were creating a
three-dimensional painting, juxtaposing one
color and shape against another.

The more defined a room's function, the harder it can be to design.

chapter eight
Functional Spaces

Paradoxically, it is often true that the clearer and more defined a room's function, the harder it is to design. Kitchens and bathrooms are often the most problematic. They should work efficiently and also add to the ambiance of the home. A similar kind of complexity arises when creating bedrooms, home offices, and libraries. In part the difficulties arise because there are so many options. Kitchens basically need to serve for storing, preparing, and, often, eating food. But in the era of trash compactors, convection ovens, dual sinks, wine coolers, multiple dishwashers, and electric plate warmers, nothing is simple anymore. And with bathrooms becoming more like home spas than just a place to shower and shave, designing a bathroom is no longer simply a matter of deciding the color of the tiles and towels.

The increased prevalence of technology in our lives—from the Internet to fax machines to cell phones to security systems—makes designing the rooms where we use these conveniences even more complicated. That is one reason why in our work, we always try to think of these as modern rooms. We do not believe in creating faux "period" rooms, hiding technology, disguising it, or pretending it doesn't exist.

For example, one of the biggest predicaments facing people when putting together a bedroom is where to put the TV. Many people feel that unless they hide it in an armoire or a cabinet, the set will be an eyesore. Yet we feel it is much more honest to proudly display the TV on a stand or table. Televisions have become sleeker and better designed over the years (no more faux wood paneling), and with the advent of flat-screen televisions, they are less bulky and easier to place in a room. Television is not going away, and with the promise of Internet access directly through the television, the set is likely to become even more central to our lives. It is silly to pretend otherwise.

In a country bedroom, a high
headboard is upholstered
with a handwoven cotton
and covered in a washable
fabric. The owner's collection of
Karl Blossfeldt photographs
hangs above.

Bedrooms are much lovelier when a seating area or a beautiful chest of drawers is the initial focus.

BEDROOMS

A bedroom is primarily for sleeping, so it is important to have the best box spring, mattress, and pillows you can afford (which need to be replaced at regular intervals). If a bedroom can't deliver a good night's sleep, then it doesn't matter if it works on a design level. The choice of a grand carved four-poster or a simple platform is purely personal. Headboards can be plain or elaborate, sleek or antique, made of wood, fabric, or parchment. The bed will influence all the other choices in the room. And of course, there should be at least three sets of high-quality sheets. Fortunately, there is a wide range of pretty sheets available today. While we still love classic white cotton and linen sheets, there are lovely patterned ones as well, and we also like pale grays, blues, and greens. But this is largely a matter of personal preference and what works best with the color scheme of the room. Most people today use duvet covers rather than bedspreads and prefer a look of fluffiness to their beds, with linens turned back, lots of pillows of various shapes, and soft blankets. Yet a more tailored look can be beautiful and in some cases may be a better choice, depending upon the mood of the room.

In a New Jersey bedroom, a 1930s German cabinet holds the television. On a scrubbed-oak desk by Dwellings sits a Jean-Michel Frank travertine lamp. The bed is draped in green voile; on either side are Austrian bronze lamps from the 1930s.

In the bedroom of our guest cottage, opposite, the bed is steel Gothic, the secretary Charles X. An antique map of Paris hangs behind the bed. A Park Avenue bedroom, below, features silver satin draperies, a Georgian secretary, and an English Regency writing table. The urns on the desk are eighteenth-century German porcelain.

If a bedroom can't deliver a good night's sleep, then it doesn't matter if it works on a design level.

Other considerations include light—some kind of blackout material at the windows is a must—and there should be lamps on both sides of the bed to allow reading. Bedside tables should be large enough to accommodate a phone, a lamp, and perhaps a carafe of water. They should also have a drawer for little necessities like eyeglasses, books, pens, paper, tissues, etc. (If there is no drawer, there should at least be a lovely box or basket large enough to store this clutter.) A bedroom also benefits from some softness on the floor. Most people when they first step out of bed prefer to place their bare feet on soft material, so an area rug near the bed or wall-to-wall carpeting is advisable.

A chair with an ottoman or a chaise allows conversations with someone in bed and another place to read and relax. If there is no separate dressing room, a vanity may be needed. Many people also like to have a desk in their bedroom and even a bookcase. Couples with children may want to create a comfortable area in their bedroom for their children to play, especially on weekend mornings. A bedroom can also be made more inviting with a stereo system and scented candles. The bedroom is the most personal room in the house and should be the most comfortable.

A country bedroom centers on a steel Directoire bed flanked by American wire lamps. The desk chair is by Jean-Charles Moreaux.

BATHROOMS

We believe bathrooms should be simple, functional, and comfortable. Although some people prefer grand fantasy bathrooms, we have never felt that the bathroom is an appropriate place for ostentation. It is a private space, and usually not huge, so we believe in devising a soft scheme, unified in color and materials, to create a room that is soothing. The most luxurious bathrooms are those in which you feel pampered and catered to, almost as if you were in a private spa, not those that have the most marble or gold.

In a bath, the paramount considerations should be lighting, ventilation, and adequate mirrors. There should be flattering ambient light but also strong task lighting for shaving or putting on makeup. A full-length mirror is a wonderful luxury, if there is adequate wall space, but a three-way mirror of some kind, hung on a wall or on the doors of a medicine cabinet, is a must. It is also helpful to have some kind of magnifying mirror handy.

If you are creating a new bathroom, keep in mind that space to move around easily is key, and try to place the toilet in a position that minimizes its importance and visibility. The tub, a place of refuge at the beginning or end of the day, makes a far more beautiful focal point. Make certain to have plenty of electrical outlets installed, and not just near the floor. Electric toothbrushes, razors, and

The most luxurious
bathrooms are those
in which you feel
pampered and
catered to . . .

The entry to a country bath is marked by an Italian Baroque painted screen. The tub is painted to look like marble. The slipper chair is by Dwellings.

hair dryers all require outlets in the proper position. Good shelves are also important, either exposed or hidden behind cabinet doors, to hold fresh towels and ample beauty supplies.

Consider the height of vanities and counters. Often these are too low, especially in the case of antique pieces, because we are taller today than a hundred years ago. Hunching over a too-low counter for a long period can be both annoying and painful. Install counters at least waist high. If you are dealing with antiques, you might want to raise them up, either by extending their legs or placing them on platforms.

Of course, a bathroom can be made even more luxurious and pampering with touches such as heated towel bars, a small TV, a clock, candles, a stereo, and a vase of fresh flowers.

All these principles apply to designing a guest bath, as well. But in addition to fresh towels and guest soaps, stock the guest bath with any items that your guests are likely to forget, including extra razors, toothbrushes, and shampoo.

In an Aspen house, a pair of Roman marble tubs center a room tiled in Moroccan-style tiles made in England. The cabinet is Spanish, the mirror is Dutch. A Jacobean bench is upholstered in an antique African textile.

In any bathroom, lighting, ventilation, and adequate mirrors should be paramount considerations.

In a Miami bath, top right, built-in cabinets provide storage. The rug is French, from the 1940s. Above: In a guest bath are a French horsehair screen and a medicine cabinet hidden behind a Dutch mirror. Right: In a Park Avenue bathroom, a fitted tub is surrounded by marble and mirrors. Opposite: Art Nouveau sconces echo the curves of the fittings of a French 1930s double sink.

In a downtown Manhattan loft a
concrete tub and custom cabinetry
create a private spa in the sky.

KITCHENS

The kitchen is one of the most-used rooms in any house or apartment and is often the most sociable, as well. Whether it's a fully equipped gourmet chef's dream or a minimal space used mainly for making coffee and microwaving frozen dinners, it should function well and fit visually with the rest of the house. Many kitchens now are hybrid spaces, used not only for cooking and eating but also as expanded family rooms or as home offices. In many urban lofts the kitchens are open to the living area. The more functions a kitchen serves, the more

If there is enough space, an island is a godsend. Some islands contain a cooktop and/or sink, but even a simple island with a counter and storage beneath will greatly help in the preparation of food and can function as a serving space for snacks and light meals. This is particularly valuable in a kitchen that is too small for a table. Even a stool at a counter will make a kitchen warmer and more inviting.

Lighting is also crucial. Abundant natural light is best, of course, but whether there are plenty of windows or none, there needs to be sufficient task lighting to permit cooking

The kitchen is often the most sociable room in the house.

important it is that it be efficient in layout, comfortable to use, and visually pleasing.

The major consideration in planning any new kitchen is the placement of stove, refrigerator, and sink within a triangle configuration. No matter how many other appliances or gadgets a kitchen contains, these three are the most frequently used. The closer they are, the more steps and time will be saved. The total length of the three legs of this triangle should total no more than 26 feet, with no single leg being shorter than 4 feet or longer than 9 feet. Aisles should be at least 42 inches wide. Also remember that the doors of the refrigerator, oven, and dishwasher when open should not interfere with each other.

and cleanup without eyestrain. Other factors to consider are a place for a chopping board near the sink, adequate pull-out drawers for pots and pans, and other drawers for dish towels, pot holders, and all the other small gadgets that inevitably accumulate in even the most minimal kitchen.

The ultimate luxury for a kitchen is to have a separate pantry large enough to hold all the supplies and cooking equipment, so that overhead cabinets aren't needed. This opens up a kitchen in wonderful ways, admitting light and air. But few kitchens are large enough to forgo overhead storage, with either cabinets or open shelving. These should be unobtrusive and functional so that the vast majority of items are within

In a Fifth Avenue kitchen, antique terra-cotta floors provide a practical surface. A collection of French apothecary jars is displayed on brackets.

easy reach. Open shelves or glass-fronted cabinets can also display collections of china, teapots, and other decorative pieces, which add charm to the room.

Space permitting, a second sink is useful. A second dishwasher is a luxury but especially useful in homes where a lot of entertaining is done. An ice machine is also helpful. Any number of innovative appliances and gadgets can be incorporated into a kitchen, from plate warmers to cappuccino machines to climate-controlled wine cellars, depending upon space and budget. But no matter how many of these are added, if the kitchen is not well laid out, it will never be a pleasure to use.

In terms of style, the kitchen should be simple and consistent with the rest of the house. We don't like "theme" kitchens or elaborate showplaces. Whether the major material is white beadboard, sleek stainless steel, or a warm wood, the kitchen should blend well with the other rooms and share a similar spirit. In smaller apartments, we try to use the same flooring material in the

The design of a kitchen should be simple and consistent with the rest of the house.

In our country house, a central island is lighted by an Austrian bronze chandelier. French doors lead to a terrace.

If a kitchen is not well laid out, it will never be a pleasure to use.

A Manhattan kitchen, above, has painted metal cabinets and a Venini hanging lamp. The Roman shades are in a checked cotton. The breakfast nook in a Gramercy Park apartment, left, has a tufted wraparound banquette and a French table. Opposite: The original fireplace is flanked by American iron finials. The bowls are Chinese bronzes.

A downtown Manhattan loft features
a fitted kitchen that is open to the
dining area. The simple steel table is
on wheels for flexibility. The chairs
are Viennese, by Josef Hoffmann.

The more functions a kitchen serves, the more important it is that it be visually pleasing.

In a midwestern house, the kitchen opens directly to a family room for entertaining. The mantel is French limestone, the mirror above it is porcelain in imitation of Persian tiles, from the early nineteenth century. All upholstery and curtains are in the same printed fabric.

kitchen as in the other rooms, so as not to break up the flow of space. The kitchen should only extend and elaborate the mood and tone of the decor, not contrast with it. Stepping into a kitchen should never be a shock or a surprise.

LIBRARIES AND HOME OFFICES

It is wonderful to live with books. Filling a room with books instantly creates a cozy, comforting atmosphere. Little else besides a comfortable chair and a lamp is needed. Having a separate room that serves as a library is ideal, but even smaller living spaces with just a corner bookcase or two will benefit from the charm books bring. Libraries are no longer rarely used sanctuaries, but multifunctional rooms. They have replaced the den and often house a home office. It is a pleasure to eat in a library, either a small intimate supper at a round table or a simple meal on a tray while watching television. A library outfitted with a bar, even a temporary one, can be the most relaxed place to hold a small cocktail party or to gather before dinner.

We prefer shelves and bookcases to be as simple as possible so that they fade into the background and let the books take center stage. This doesn't mean, however, that the bookcases need to be of dark wood or metal. We have done very beautiful libraries in white, for example. But the focus should not be on the structure or decoration of the

Filling a room with books instantly creates a cozy, comforting atmosphere.

In a library overlooking Central Park, custom shelves are covered in silk velvet. A silver-plated ladder rolls on a steel rod. The painted chairs are Italian, from the early eighteenth century. The lantern in the hall is Louis XV.

bookcases. Intermingling books with beautiful pieces of pottery or ceramics, framed drawings, silver objects, or other personal collections will draw the eye to the shelves. And remember, bookcases need not fill a wall. We like to use étagères and freestanding cases. Low bookcases break up a space or permit the hanging of artworks.

A comfortable place to sit is essential. Club chairs are ideal, either in leather or in velvet or mohair chenille. We prefer using several loveseats, rather than a large sofa, to further the sense of intimacy in the room. Provide plenty of surfaces, such as small

people set up an office off the kitchen or in a space adjacent to the bedroom. And even though the office requires a phone, fax, answering machine, and computer, it doesn't have to look cold or commercial. As high-tech equipment becomes better designed, it becomes easier to integrate these pieces into the overall mood of the room. The other requirements are a large work surface, enough drawers to hold bills, papers, and other files, and a good chair, designed to support the back for extended periods. But these items don't have to be ordered from an office supply store. A variety

Shelves and bookcases should be as simple as possible, so the books take center stage.

tables, an ottoman, or a low bookcase, on which to place drinks, books, magazines, eyeglasses, etc. There must be adequate lamps for reading, of course, but the atmosphere will be greatly enhanced by a chandelier or lanterns or other hanging fixtures or wall sconces, which add charm. A desk or worktable allows the library to be used for writing letters and paying bills, and it is a great place for the display of family photos and other personal mementos.

A library is an ideal place to set up a home office. But a home office doesn't necessarily require a separate room. Any small space with adequate privacy and quiet can be adapted for use as an office. Many

of well-designed and attractive pieces are now available, and an antique desk or chair may prove just as efficient and comfortable as a new one. What is most important is deciding how often and for what purposes you will use the office, and thus what kind of space and equipment you will need. A home office must be efficient and functional, but it should also be a recognizable part of the home.

In a Fifth Avenue apartment, architecturally integrated bookcases are reached with an English ladder. A Louis XVI writing table is paired with Directoire Klismos chairs.

A home office must be efficient, but it should also be a recognizable part of the home.

Opposite: In a New York apartment, a built-in oak desk, a pair of American gooseneck lamps, and a wicker chair reflect the spareness of the view beyond. Right: Classic Mies van der Rohe chairs, a steel table, and a drawing by Richard Serra in a corner used as an office. Below: Contemporary furniture and an assemblage of architectural fragments.

Right: In a more elaborate home office, oak paneling and shelves highlight a view of Central Park. The drawings are by Brice Marden.

It is the
personal touches
that bring a
room to life.

chapter nine
Finishing Details

A room can be well laid out and full of lovely furniture, yet still seem inert. It is the finishing details, the personal touches, the small arrangements of beautiful and beloved objects, that bring a room to life. A well-thought-out assemblage makes the difference between a beautiful still life and just another pile of stuff. Think of the creation of these tableaux not as a problem, but as an opportunity to express your personal style.

There is one primary rule in composing an arrangement of objects, whether on a mantel, side table, or bookcase: Understand the mood and spirit of the room itself. Not every object can be used in every situation. For example, in a formal room full of rich silks and velvets, you would choose items with a more refined sensibility, such as wedding silver, crystal bowls, and fine china. In a rustic country house, all you might need is a collection of pebbles, rocks, and fossils or an unusual piece of driftwood. While there are some objects, like finely woven baskets or pottery, that can work in almost any environment, it is important to select only those objects that will enhance the overall effect of the room.

Editing is your best tool. Always pare down; don't fill up a space. If objects don't have either intrinsic beauty or some personal resonance, they shouldn't be on display. And remember, a beautiful lamp that brings warm light into a room is the best accessory and should take precedence over all other objects.

Always try to arrange objects by color and shape. Brought together, they will take on greater power and significance than they have individually. Each piece in the group will reinforce the other, as long as they are similar in spirit. Don't attempt to make dramatic contrasts. Don't put a Navajo basket next to a cut-crystal vase, or a piece of rustic pottery next to china. These objects will be at war with each other.

On the mantel of a country home, an array of small wooden books and a Karl Blossfeldt photograph in an antique gilt bamboo frame. Opposite: In our Manhattan apartment, a shagreen secretary by Jacques Adnet holds a plaster vase by Giacometti and antique Chinese marble oranges. The mask is Pre-Columbian Colima.

We learned long ago from the British decorator David Hicks, the original master of tablescapes and the placement of accessories, the power of assemblages. Hicks would simply line up collections—of boxes, stone animals, pieces of porcelain—on a table or shelf. The collection would take on much greater impact than when the elements were scattered about the room. Not only did the presentation showcase the interests of the room's owner, but the rigor of their geometric presentation, carefully lined up in rows, also helped to undercut any excess whimsy that might be inherent in the objects themselves.

We love symmetry, and it is key to our style of decorating. But sometimes you need to break the line and deliberately use asymmetry. This is something the greatest artists have always understood. Too much balance, objects too regular in the rhythm of their placement and too evenly spaced, will soon bore the eye. Deliberate asymmetry livens up an arrangement, makes it seem not so obvious. And while it is wonderful to have pairs of objects—lamps or urns or vases or candlesticks—it is not always the best choice to place them on opposite sides of a mantel or on matching tables on each side of the sofa. Often, putting the two objects together and counterpointing them with a single different and larger piece on the opposite side makes a stronger statement. Pieces need not be the same to balance each other. Visual weight is what counts.

Try to create vignettes, almost as if you were telling a story. Use objects of varying

A collection takes on much greater impact when assembled, not scattered about the room.

An Indian sandstone relief and antique Turkish fabric on the table create a backdrop for a collection of metalwork. Opposite: An array of Islamic iron bowls and containers backed by Turkish engravings.

heights, to create a rhythm across a mantel or on a table. Don't be afraid to experiment. Play with scale as well, and don't underestimate the power of small objects. Whereas one small object might be overwhelmed, a series of eight can be a delightful surprise on a tall mantel, for example, setting up an unexpected syncopation. Look at the work of master painters. Chardin and Morandi certainly understood the appeal and the power of simple, small objects.

Don't underestimate the freshness that an unexpected object will bring. Any object that you love and find beautiful, no matter its provenance or original purpose, can be

right placed next to one of wicker, for example, or gilt next to leather.

Keep revisiting and editing the objects on display. Many people are intimidated by having to create tablescapes or arrangements and keep objects in very precise places. Some decorators tell of clients who photograph every surface so that the arrangements will be duplicated to the smallest detail. Yet this is antithetical to the purpose of having beautiful objects on display. If their placement never changes, you will eventually stop seeing them. Therefore, feel free to move and modify your displays. In the summer you might want to replace

Pieces need not be the same to balance each other.

used to beautify a room. You don't need expensive items. A straw basket filled with green apples makes a wonderful focal point. Stone objects and bronze bowls bring a sense of permanence to a room, but folk-art birds and spongeware pottery can have the same effect. What is important is that objects share a consistency of shape and form and a similarity of spirit.

The most personal objects are family photographs, and for this reason they are best displayed in a bedroom or library. They will look wonderful on a dresser, on a side table, or interspersed with books in a bookcase. They should be framed simply and in compatible style. A silver frame won't look

pottery with crystal and glass pieces that will reflect the abundant sunlight. Move objects to different rooms to see them in a fresh light, or simply put them away for six or eight months so that when you pull them out again, it will be as if you are seeing them for the first time.

The same general rules apply to bringing flowers and plants into a room. Living things always provide a sense of vitality to a room. Also add color and texture to a room through the use of pillows on sofas and

In our guest cottage, a circular Roman marble bas relief echoes the round window. A collection of ax handles is flanked by a French sculpture and a Dwellings lamp.

chairs. Pillows are an easy and immediate way to change the decor, to bring in unexpected color, pattern, and texture. If you have a beautiful cinnabar box, for example, amplify its presence with pillows of the same color. Pillows can provide a quick seasonal change, as well. White linen covers for the summer, replaced by dark damask ones in the fall and winter, will have a dramatic impact.

Beautifully framed mirrors add instant glamour and reflect and heighten the light in the room, whether it is sunlight or candlelight. Artwork enriches a room immeasurably. If you can't afford paintings or sculpture, consider investing in a tapestry or a series of photographs or prints—even old maps or beautiful illustrations taken from old books can be unique and eye-catching.

The general rule is to hang pictures at eye level, but we tend to place them slightly higher, usually about two or three inches. We have found that this adds drama to the room. Hanging works at this level causes your eye to be pitched slightly higher and makes the ceiling seem taller and the room more airy. We also love to double- and triple-hang compatible pieces. A series of prints or photographs identically framed and hung together is always striking. The works will have much greater impact than if hung individually. For small works, another option is to place them on a table, or leaning on a shelf, interspersed among books.

This way they won't be overwhelmed by too much wall space and can even be picked up for close inspection.

Setting a table provides another opportunity for self-expression. The rules of formal dining have been relaxed, and this applies particularly to the table. You no longer need a formal tablecloth or matching silver and elaborate sets of china. Often simple straw mats are all you need. Feel free to mix heirlooms with modern pieces. Even stemware is not required. Wine can be served in on-the-rocks glasses or small decorative tumblers from Istanbul or Venice, for example. You can replace flowers as the centerpiece with a small topiary or even a collection of objects. Or instead of a centerpiece, place several small vases of flowers around the table. Candles are a must, but you don't need tall candlesticks or candelabra. Small votives or hurricane lamps add a lovely glow. Think of the table setting as a chance for innovation and an opportunity to bring out pretty items that you rarely use. This will make you appreciate these items all the more. And breaking the rules at the table will encourage you to rethink the other displays throughout your home.

The more personal your home, the more reflective of your style and interests, the more you will enjoy spending time there. And paradoxically, the more personal the house, the more welcoming it is to friends and family.

In a Connecticut country house, simple objects add richness. A large apothecary jar holds fruit and glass floats, and simple tin artists' forms create a still-life on the mantel. The original pine floors of the sculptural staircase become a focus in themselves.

In a Manhattan bath,
natural sponges on a
French bronze gueridon
become a sculptural
display.

Don't underestimate
the freshness that
an unexpected
object will bring.

In the entry to our New York apartment, an Emilio Terry mirror, a Man Ray photograph, and a Greek fragment under the watchful eye of a French eighteenth-century neoclassical bust. The marble console is American.

Keep revisiting and editing objects on display. If their placement never changes,

The entry of the London townhouse of a young family features a nineteenth-century hand-painted leather screen, opposite, over a Directoire mahogany console. In the living room, right and below, a tray on the ottoman holds an ancient stone sculpture and a simple bowl of eggs.

you will eventually stop seeing them.

Your home should be as rich and varied as the life you live within it.

chapter ten
Change

Change is inevitable, and yet people fear it and attempt to forestall it, rather than welcome and plan for it. People marry or divorce. Children are born or move out of the house. Jobs change. Circumstances alter. Our needs and desires evolve . . . and our homes should reflect those changes.

Don't be afraid to change your home. The changes can be small, temporary, or seasonal, yet they can have a major impact. Just replacing heavy winter drapes and slipcovers with light linen ones to celebrate the arrival of summer will have a wonderfully beneficial effect on your home. You might rehang or rotate the artworks in your home to make them vivid to your eye once again. Or paint a room a different color.

Sometimes the changes can be major. You may move to a larger or smaller home or combine households with someone you love. Your home needs to reflect that different reality, and the new way you live.

Change need not be dictated only by different circumstances. If your eye has grown tired of your home, if it no longer pleases you, that is reason enough to rethink it. People may spend thousands of dollars updating their wardrobes regularly, yet never think about updating their homes. Perhaps they hesitate because they are not sure how to proceed or think it is too much trouble. Yet the place where you live and entertain is even more of a reflection of your style than your clothes and deserves at least as much thought and expense.

Even the most successful decor will age or become dated or worn. And as your eye and tastes shift, you will want to express your new interests and awareness in your home. We have redone elements of our country house three or four times and have changed our city apartment as well. Some of our best clients have redone their homes several times. We hope that their example, seen on these pages, will inspire you.

Changes can
be small, temporary,
or seasonal, yet
they can have a
major impact.

Living in your home is an ongoing, organic process, and its decoration should reflect that. Your home should be as rich and varied as the life you live within it. And if you make your home beautiful, and continue to fill it with objects and people that you love, then it will always remain the place that gives you the greatest pleasure in life.

If your eye has grown tired of your home, if it no longer pleases you, that is reason enough to rethink it.

Two incarnations of the same Southampton living room: The original design, above, featured American wicker and Windsor chairs and English ceramic plant stands.

Three years later, a redesign brought in chairs by Josef Hoffmann, a Mies van der Rohe glass table, and an eighteenth-century Dutch painted console. The rare basalt pottery on the mantel is a consistent element.

In the bedroom's original guise, the American iron bed was covered with a crochet coverlet. The armoire is Egyptian Revival. On the mantel were an American painting and a collection of wood books.

After the redesign, the walls were painted goldenrod, a checked wall-to-wall carpet was installed, and a tailored bed covering was added. Karl Blossfeldt photographs in gilt frames were placed on the mantel. The plant stand is French neoclassical.

Continuing evolution: The room in its second incarnation contains a Dwellings sofa and club chairs. The overscaled vase is papier-mâché, made for a theatrical production. The black lacquered cabinet is Austrian. On the stenciled floors are antique American hooked and crewelwork rugs.

The latest, if not final, version, right and opposite: The sitting room now contains a Mies van der Rohe leather daybed, a leather wing chair, a custom Cubistic wood table, and a Dwellings sofa. On the walls are a Richard Serra drawing and a collection of dried Mediterranean algae in ebonized frames.

PHOTO CREDITS

INDEX

and stenciled walls, 72, 150; and stripes, 142, *148–49*

change: in home, 27, 212–18, *214, 215, 216, 217, 218*; and object arrangement, 201

color: and bathrooms, 169; and bedrooms, *86*, 94; and dining rooms, *92, 96–97*; and fabric, 106, 150, *153*, 154, *155*; and floors, 95; and furniture, *91*, 98, 103, *103*, 106, *109*, 124; harmonizing of, 84, 90; inspiration for, *85*; as integral to material, 90; and libraries, *93*, 94; monochromatic color schemes, 13, 14, 70, 72, 75, 88–89, 94, 98, 106; and object arrangement, *11*, 194, *195*; and personal style, 34, *39*, 41; and pillows, 154, 201–02; principles of, 84; and rugs, *45*, 84, 98, *100–101*, 134, 139; strong colors, 94, 98, *102*, 103, *103*; and texture, 87, *88–89*, 90, 98; unusual colors, 90, 94; and upholstery, 72, *94*, *96–97*, 98; and walls, 90, 94, *95*, *96–97*, 98, 142; and warm/cool polarities, 87; white with shots of bright color, 98, *99*

D

desires: and inspirations bulletin board, 27; scrutinizing, 22, 27, 30, 34

dining rooms: and color, *92*, *96–97*; and floor plans, 44, *62*; and furniture, 109; living/dining room, *74*, 75–78, *75*, *76*, *77*; and needs, 14, *19*; and

personal style, 27, *32, 33*; and table settings, 202

down sofas, 122

dyed plaster walls, 142, *143*

E

economics: and needs, 27; and style, 13–14; and walls, 142. *See also* budget

editing: importance of, 14; and object arrangement, 194, 201, 209; and personal style, 22

electrical outlets, 58, 169, 172

entertaining room example, 78, *79, 80, 81*

entry halls, 14, *16–17, 28*, 79, 120, *137*

F

fabric: and bedrooms, *156, 157*; and change, 212; and color, 106, 150, *153*, 154, *155*; and floor plans, 44; and object arrangement, 194; and pattern, 78, *107*, 150, *152, 153*, 154; and personal style, 34; and pillows, 150, 154; and surfaces, 150–57; and upholstered furniture, 117, *118–19*, 122, 150, 154; and walls, 142, *143, 153*

façade of house, *12, 13*

family photographs, 201

finishing details, 194–209

floor plans: and bedrooms, 44, 47, *57*, 58, *67*; and flexibility, 44, *51, 52–53*, 58, *62, 63*; and function, 44, 47, 70; and furniture, 54, *55, 56*, 58, *60, 61*, 106; and libraries, 44, *48, 63*; and living rooms, 44, *45*,

46–47, 51, 52–53, 60, 61, 64–65, 66; and room proportions, 44, 47, 49, 54, 56, 58; and traffic patterns, 49, 54

floors: and color, 95; and function, 134, 139; and kitchens, *179*, 181, 187; optical-illusion flooring, *28*, *137*; and upholstery, *138. See also* rugs

flowers, 201, 202

function: and bathrooms, 10, 27, 160, 169–77, *171, 172–73, 174, 175, 176–77*; and bedrooms, 44, 160, *162–63*, 164, 165–69, *166, 167, 168*; defining nature of, 160; and floor plans, 44, 47, 70; and floors, 134, 139; and furniture, 70, 72, 106, 109, 113, 114; of home, 10, 22; and home offices, 10, 160, 188, *190, 191*; importance of, 14, 70; and kitchens, 10, 14, 27, 160, 178–85, *179, 180–81, 182, 183, 184–85*, 187; and libraries, 27, 160, *186*, 187–88, *187, 189*; and needs, 27

furniture: adapting older pieces, 114, 117; and bedrooms, *110, 111*, 113, *129*; and color, *91*, 98, 103, *103*, 106, *109*, 124; and floor plans, 54, *55, 56*, 58, *60, 61*, 106; and floors, *138*; and function, 70, 72, 106, 109, 113, 114; guidelines for grouping furniture, 54, 58, 75, 78, 114, 122, 124, *125*, 127; and libraries, *120, 121, 126, 127*; and living rooms, 109, 113, 114, *116, 127*; and mixing styles and periods, 114, *115*; and personal style, 34, *40*;

Since founding their partnership more than twenty years ago,
Stephen Sills and James Huniford have been recognized as being
among America's most creative interior designers. The clients of their
firm, Sills Huniford Associates, have ranged from members of the
Rockefeller family to Vera Wang, Jane Pratt, and Tina Turner.
Their projects have appeared in numerous publications, including
*Architectural Digest, Elle Décor, House & Garden, World of Interiors,
Vogue,* and the *New York Times.* This is their first book.